Virginia Colonial Abstracts
Vol. II

Northumberland County Records
1652-1655

Containing Abstracts from:

Court Order Book #2
20th Sept. 1652 – 20th Oct. 1655

Record Book #14
20th Sept. 1652 – 20th Aug. 1655

By:
Beverly Fleet
Box 161 West End Station
Richmond, Virginia

This volume was reproduced from
An 1948 edition located in the
Publishers Private Library,
Greenville, South Carolina

All rights reserved. No part of this publication
may be reproduced, stored in a retrieval system,
transmitted in any form, posted on to the web
in any form or by any means without the
prior written permission of the publisher.

Please direct all correspondence and orders to:

www.southernhistoricalpress.com
or
SOUTHERN HISTORICAL PRESS, Inc.
PO BOX 1267
375 West Broad Street
Greenville, SC   29601
southernhistoricalpress@gmail.com

Originally published: Richmond, 1948
Reprinted by:
Southern Historical Press, Inc.
Greenville, SC
ISBN #0-89308-942-7
All rights Reserved.
Printed in the United States of America

Preface.

Now for Northumberland. In considering these records Court Order Book #2 was selected. This book being so difficult that the valuable data it contained was not available, as a whole, even to students who are able to consult it. Sufficient to say, that with a magnifying glass constantly at hand, it has at times, taken me more than a day to transcribe a single entry. Perhaps others are swifter than I, but there is no such thing as glancing through and hurriedly picking out the items that refer to any particular subject or family. These books are badly mutilated, the ink faded and the 17th Century Court Hand so fine and small that the individual letters are hardly as large as this type. For a little relief from this I would occasionally look through other items, and in this way came upon Record Book #14, covering the same period and with many entries that dovetailed in with Order Book #2. It seemed more satisfactory to give a shorter period than to attempt to cover a longer and leave half unwritten. Now having complained and explained, I will add that these records were to me, intensely interesting.

It did not take very long to find out that these records were highly improper in the Victorian sense. Not ambitious to purvey that class of literature described by a President of Yale as 'deplorable', I hesitated. But then considering that my readers were not as young and innocent as they should be, it seemed best to let them have it. The whole purpose of this work being to give what I could of the original records, so that the student might judge for himself, rather than to have to accept the deductions of others. But I must confess that the cruelty and general vulgarity of our ancestors from Northumberland was shocking. Thank goodness there was some comedy, even if unconcious on their part. One of the modern delights of the Archives Department is to see a genealogist, who is positive that she is a lady, squirm and apologise while untangling Northumberland lines.

Again I must express my appreciation for the consideration and help (pronounced in Virginia 'hep') given by the invaluable Mr. Morgan Poitiaux Robinson, Miss Estelle Bass and Mrs. James Claiborne Pollard in the Department of Archives. I just could not do it, and certainly would not want to without their aid. The kindly attitude of many friends known and unknown in regard to the Lancaster Abstracts, the first volume in the series, has been most deeply appreciated, particularly that of our country's great universities. That has indeed been sufficient reward.

Beverley Fleet.
Box 161. West End Station,
Richmond, Virginia.

Northumberland County, Virginia.
Court Order Book #2.

page 1.

The 20th of September 1652.

Present.

Coll John Mottrom   Mr Wm Mosly
Lt.Col Geo ffletcher   Mr John Hallowes
Mr Tho Speke   Mr Walter Brodhurst
Mr John Trussell   Mr Sam Smith
              Mr Nicho Morris

Lt Coll Geo ffletcher was sworn a Comr

Mr Speke   Whereas it doth appear unto the Court by the oath
agt   of Mr Tho Speke that Henry Barnes doth owe unto the
Henry Barnes   said Mr Speke one thousand pounds of tobaco upon
his Estate   accot and the said Barnes is secretly departed this
                    county the Court doth therefore order that an attach-
ment shal issue out of that Court against the estate of the said Barnes
whatever the pltiff can find is in satisfaction of the said debt with
charges of Court.

Tho Keene   Whereas it doth appear unto the Court that Henry
agt   Barnes doth owe unto Thomas Keene ffive hund and
Henry Barnes   twenty six pounds of Tobco upon accot to the - - -
his Estate   (page mutilated) - - the said - - Keene did then take
                    his oath and said Barnes had secretly departed this
County - - date thereof ordrd that an attachment shal issue out of this
Court agst the estate of the said Barnes if he can find any after Mr
Thomas Spekes debt of a thousand pounds of tobaco that ord of Court is
satisfied - - in satisfaction of the debt wth charges of Court

John Powell   Whereas it doth appear unto the Court That
agst   Edward Hudson doth owe unto John Powell - - - of
Edward Hudson   toboco - - by Bills - the said Hudson being secretly
his Estate   departed this County The Court doth therefore Ordr
                    that the said Powell shal have an attachment agt the
estate of the said Hudson in the first - - for - - satisfaction of the
said debt with - -

Mr Hallowes Att of (Entry mutilated) "Whereas it doth appear unto the
- - Brackitt   Court und'r the hand of Michael - - - -that the
agt   said - - - doth owe unto - - two thousand and one
- - - - Att of -   hundred and eight Pounds of Tobo'r - - by two sev-
- - -   -   eral Bills the Court doth therefore order that John
                    Walton Attur of the said - - - shall make paymt of
the said debt unto Mr John Hallowes atty of the said Brackitt by the 20th

Order Book #2. 20th Sept. 1652. page 1.

of Novem next with the charges of Court - - - always if - - that if the said Walton can - - any acquittance that - - of the debt is satisfyed it and also allowed - - this order - - "

Mr Hallowes
agt
Edw Thompson
and Rich Hawkins

(Entry mutilated) Edward Thompson for himself and Richard Hawkins ack a judgement for these - - six hundred and fifty pounds - - unto John Hallowes with charges - -.

- - - Brodhurst
Tho Gossard
agt
John Essex

"Whereas it doth appear unto the Court that Jo Essex does owe unto Mr Tho Gossard Administrator of Henry Brooke deceased the sum of " 265 lb. of tobo. The Court orders Essex to forthwith make payment "with forbearance and charges of Court unto Mr Walter Brodhurst x x."

Richard Hawkins
agt
Rich Turney

"Whereas it doth appear unto the Court that Mr Rich Turney doth owe unto Richard Hawkins" 340 lbs of tobo. "by Bill the Court doth therefore that the said Mr Turney shall make payment x x."

John Walton
agt
Edward Hudson's
security

" Whereas Edward Hudson did receive a keg and a bag of nailes of John Waltons wife to be delivered to John Walton the Court doth therefore order that James Willis security for the said Hudson (who has socretly departed this county) shall pay unto the said Walton " 350 lbs. tobo. and cask "in full satisfaction of the goods aforesaid by the 10th of Novem next with charges of Court x x and the Court doth further order that the said Willis shall take soe much of the estate of the said Hudsons (if he can find any after John Powell is satisfied) as will satisfy the said 350 lb. tobo x x x."

Mr Walter Brodhurst
Attur of Mr Lewis
Burrell
agt
Mr Richard Turney

"Whereas it doth appear unto the Court that Mr Richard Turney doth owe unto Mr Lewis Burrell" 2800 lbs "of good sweete fatt meat and caske without heads or feete well dressed and salted to be paid at the dwelling house of the said Burrell and twelve Barrels of good Indian Corne by Bill The Court doth therefore order that the said Mr Turney shall make payment of said debt with charges of Court unto the said Mr Burrell or unto Mr Walter Brodhurst his Attur by the 20th of Novem next x x."

Corbet Pod
agt
Mr Jo Rosier

To, next Court.
This name appears to be Corbet Podle.

Order Book #2. 20th September 1652. page 1.

Robert Wyard
his cert for Land
	"According to sufficient proof made to this Court there is due to Robert Wyard 150 acres for the transportation of these persons following into this colony vizt:
	    Michael Phillips
	    Richard Hewes
	    Edward Dunkly "

20th September 1652. page 2.

Henry Rayner constable for Chickacone	"The Court doth appoint Henry Rayner to be constable for Chickacone for this year following and that he take his oath forthwith before a Comr"
Thomas Phillips agt Mr Turney	" Mr Richard Turney doth ack a Judgmt for the paymt of 1100 lb tobo and caske unto Thomas Phillips x x"
John Dennis Admr of John Dennis	Court order that John Dennis have comm of the Admr of the estate of John Dennis deceased.
Mr John Hallowes agt William Lewes	Lewes owing Hallowes 1985 lb. tobo. ordered to pay.
Tho Youlle agt Corbett Podle	Podle owing Youlle 700 lb. tobo. ordered to pay.
Mr Walt Brodhurst agt Tho Hawkins	To next Court
James Claughton agt Mr Nath Pope	Referred to next Court on Mr Pope's absence.
Mr Tho Speke agt Geo Watts	Watts acks Judgmt in Court for pmt of 1200 lb of tobo and cask to Speke.
Seth ffoster agt Henry Hurst	Hurst owing Foster 698 lb. of tobo. the Court orders payment by Nov. 20th.
Mr John Hallowes agt James Claughton	Claughton makes over his whole crop of tobo. to Mr Hallowes

Order Book #2. 20th Sept. 1652. page 2.

Richard Hawkins
agt
Thomas Hawkins

"Whereas it appears unto the Court by the oaths of Edward Thomson and Isaac Knight that Thomas Hawkins should deliver unto Richard Hawkins two as good cows and calves as he the said Thomas Hawkins received in exchange of Richard Hawkins The Court doth order that the said Thomas Hawkins shall make good and deliver unto the said Richard Hawkins two good cows and two calves or els the same cattle again within these ten days and with charges of Court x x "

Thos Coggin
agt
John Gresham

To next Court.

Tho Youlle
his cert for Land
following into this

"According to sufficient proofs made before this Court there is due to Thomas Youlle Two hundred acres of Land for transportation of those persons colony: Vizt:
John Cleows (Clews ?)
John Cammell
John Wilson
Marga Posley "

Wm Linsey
agt
Tho Hawkins

"The Court doth order that Wm Linsey shall serve Wm Reynolds but fower years according to the Indenture and no longer though Thomas Hawkins hath sold him for five years "

Robert Smith
agt
Tho Wilsford

Wilsford owing Smith 974 lb. tobo. ordered to pay before Nov. 20th.

Lt Coll Geo ffletcher
com on Mr Armorers estate

Lt Coll George ffletcher to have commission of administration on estate of Mr John Armorer Clerke deceased.

Tho Browne
agt
Jo Waddy

To next Court, defendt not appearing.

Andrew Munroe
his cert for
Land

According to sufficient proofs x x there is due to Andrew Monroe 100 acres of Land for the transportation of these persons following into this colony:
Vizt: John Wright
           Andrew Edenborough

page 3.

Mr John Hallowes
agt
ffrancis Gray

"Whereas Mr John Hallowes did inform the Court that ffrancis Gray hath in his possession a heifer and has - - of the estate of John Hampton deceased the Court doth therefore order That if ffrancis Gray doe not make it appear by the next Court that John Hampton gave the said

Order Book #2. September 20th 1652. page 3.

heifer in his life time to the sone of the said ffrancis Gray and that the said ffrancis Gray was possessed of the heifer in the life time of the said Hampton That then Mr Hallowes shall take the said heiffer with her - - into his possession as Administrator of John Hampton deceased And that a Copy of this ordr be sent to ffrancis Gray"

Mr John Hallowes
agt   -
Wm Bedlam

"Whereas it doth appear unto the Court that William Bedlam and his security doe owe unto Mr John Hallowes" 2670 lb. of tobo., Bedlam is ordered to pay by 20th Nov.

Note: While modern London may have a happy hypocrite in the person of Lord George Hell we have here in Northumberland our earlier and more authentic William. B.F.

Wm Haldish
his cert for
Land

250 acres due for transportation of following:
    David May
    Makum Thomson
    Henry Stuart
    Robert Anderson
    Henry Johnson

Hugh Lee
agt
John Squibb

Squibb owing Lee 452 lb. tobo ordered to pay

Coll John Mottrom
agt
Ralph Horsley

"Whereas it doth appear unto the Court that Ralph Horsly doth owe for security of John Kelly 1280 lb of tobaco and caske for a thousand pounds of Tobaco unto Coll John Mottrom " the Court orders payment by Nov 20th.

Ralph Horsley
agt
John Kelly

Kelly owing Horsley 759 lbs. tobo and cask for 1000 lbs. tobo. which he paid Coll Mottrom for Kelly, the Court orders payment.

Edward Thompson
agt
Mrs Marga Brent

20 Sept 1653 I
acknowledge to have
rec'd full satis-
faction of this
Order of Court
Edward Tomson
Test T Wilsford

"Whereas it doth appear unto the Court by the testi- mony of Mr John Hallowes that there was an Order of Mary-Land Court issued agt Mrs Margaret Brent for the paymt of two Cowes and two Calves two years aged or thereabouts unto the children of Thomas Butler and that the said Mr Hallowes took out - - agt her and she promised to pay then on this side and did not The Court doth therefore order that the said Mrs Brent shall deliver unto Edward Tomson at his now dwelling house for the use of the said children two good cowes two yearlings one male the other female by the next Court with charges of Court els -- or all femaless if she please "

Order Book #2. September 20th 1652. page 3.

Rice Maddox
agt
Coll John Mottrom

Mottrom owing Maddox 300 lb. tobo. ordered to pay.

Mr Jacob Cotansaw
agt
Mr Turney

To next Court.

Mr Rich Turney
agt
Tho Wilsford

"The Court doth order that the 330 lb. of tobaco attached in the hands of Tho Wilsford being the estate of Capt Wm Knight and due unto Mr Richard Turney from the said Knight shall be paid unto the said Mr Turney by the 20th of Novem next with charges of Court x x"

Tho Youlle
agt
Geo Watts

Watts owing Youlle 501 lbs of tobo and "a half and five Barrolls of Indian Corne" is ordered to pay by Nov. 20.

Wm Thomas
agt
Simon Richardson

"The Court doth Ordr that Simon Richardson shall make an acknowledgement in Court that he hath done Wm Thomas wrong in scandalizing of him and taking away his good name from him wch was accordingly done by the said Richardson in Court And the Court doth further order that the said Richardson shall pay unto the said Thomas Three hundred pounds of Tobaco and Caske by the 20th of Novem next in full satisfaction of the said words soe spoken by the said Richardson with charges of Court x x "

Order Book #2. 20th September 1652. page 4.

John Haney attur
of Matth Bassett
agt
Mr Rich Turney

Turney owing Bassett 300 lb. tobo. ordered to pay by November 25th.

John Haney attur
of Matth Bassett
agt
Mr Jo Trussell

Referred to next Court at Mr Trussell's motion.

John Haney attur
of Mr Wm Whitby
agt
Mr Jo Trussell

Referred to next Court at Mr Trussell's motion.

Order Book #2. 20th September 1652. page 4.

Mr Tho Speke his cert for Land	"According to sufficient proofs made to the Court there is due to Mr Thomas Speke 300 acres of Land for the transportation of these persons following into this Colony Vizt:

                        Reynold Young   James Vallins
                        John Tomson   James Colsecom (?)
                        John Marshall   Charles Rowse

This Cert was made in Wm Cocks name and delivered unto him by Mr Spekes owne order "

Mr George Colclough
his cert for Land
	100 acres due for the transp. of the following:
	       Tho Brunton
	       Walter Donne

Mr Richard Turney
his cert for Land
	250 acres due for the transpt. of the following:
	       Tho Roberts
	       Tho Jones
	       Nath Hunt
	       Mary Griggs
	       John Jrice (sic) (Grice ?)

Ralph Horsly attur of Miles Cooke agt Arthur Branch	Case referred to next Court.

Note: If there is any connection between this person and the prominent and well liked Richmond family it has not been shown by the Branch genealogists. Miss Bass, of the Archives Department, a descendant of the Henrico family should know if anyone would, but cannot identify him. However we shall see later that this Arthur can well stand on his own feet as a manly peace-maker. B.F.

Tho Hawkins agt Wm Reynolds	Reynolds owing Hawkins 250 lb. tobo. ordered to pay by Nov. 20th.
John Danby agt Mr Sam Smith and Tho Wilsford	"Whereas it doth appear unto the Court that the shoriff and the clerke of this county did neglect their offices in not arresting of Edward Hudson at the suite of John Danby The Court doth therefore order that the said Mr Sam Smith and Tho

Wilsford shall make paymt of 225 pounds of tabacco a peice in full satisfaction of the said Danbys bill by the 20th of Novem next unto the said Danby els execution "

Thomas Hawkins agt John Ingram	A jury awards that the pltf. (Hawkins) pay to the deft. (Ingram) 350 lb. tobo thus: "100 lb tobo for 6 days work performed in the said Hawkins employment and 250 for a boate and 2 men 5 days

the Journey being occasioned by a causeless suite To be paid by the 20th of Novem next"

Order Book #2. 20th September 1652. page 4.

Jonathan Steping
agt
Tho Hawkins

"In the suite depending betweene Jonathan Steping and Thos Hawkins wee do award that the said Tho Hawkins shall by the 10th day of Novem next satisfye to the said Stepping in full satisfaction of the said Steppings demands one sute of good broadcloth two good Lockram (sic) shirts one pair of new shooes and new stockings and ffower hundred pounds of tabaco in caske x x"

Wm Reynolds
agt
Tho Hawkins

"In the sute depending between Wm Reynolds pltf and Thomas Hawkins Deft wee award that" the deft. pay to pltf. one hhd. of tobo. by 20th of Nov.

"In witnes that these are our severall awards wee have sett to our hands the 21th of Septem 1652."

John Haney	Jo Bradshaw	Edward Thomson
Tho Hales his mke	Symo: Richardson	Tho Brewer mke
John Eacles	Jo Dennis his mke	Jo Kent his mke
John Gresham	Wm Cocke	Matt Rhoden

Order Book #2. 25th of November 1652. page 5.

"At a Court held for the County of Northumberland x x the 25th of Novem 1652

Present
    Collonel John Mottrom   Mr Nath Pope
    Mr Tho Speke   Majr Tho Baldridge
    Mr John Trussell   Mr Walter Brodhurst
    Mr Wm Presly   Mr Sam Smith
        Mr Nicho Morris "

Caption mutilated.
- - given to
John Peare

"The Court doth order upon John Peares petition that he shall have for this year two pounds of Tobaco per poll throughout the County for his pre- (present) reliefe and maintenance till further ord be taken for him "

Note: This type of entry does not mean that this person wasnecessarily a pauper. On the contrary it may mean that he was disabled in the defence of the early settlement. One would rather assume the latter since this was the first case considered by the Court. B.F.

Gray Clare
Mr Hollowes
Mr Ashton
ffreake and Smith
100 lb. tobo

"Whereas it doth apper unto the Court ffrancis Gray Richard Clare Mr John Hallowes Mr Charles Ashton Wm ffreake and Herbert Smith have each one of them killed a Wolfe The Court doth therefore order that every one of them shall have one hundred pounds of Tobaco paid them by the Collector in their severall limitts for the levy of this year"

Order Book #2. 25th November 1652. page 5.

Simon Richardson agt Wm Thomas	The Court having issued an order against Richardson, on Sept. 20th, for pmt of 300 lb. tobo on Nov. 20th, Richardson petitions that no execution be issued until the next Court.
Hugh ffouch agt Charles Williams	Order against Williams' estate for tobo due Fouch and for a debt of 970 lb of tobo, owed by Williams to Mr Thomas Speke and guaranteed by Fouch. "The said Williams secretly departed this county and hath taken no course for the satisfaction of his said debts".
Mr Wm Presly agt Jeremy Cooper	Cooper owing Presly 200 lb. tobo. is ordered to pay forthwith.
Willm Presly agt Ann Smith	"Whereas it doth appear unto the Court by the testimony of John Bailes Elizabeth Bailes and John Ranon that Ann Smith hath spoken scandalous words and speeches agt Mr Wm Presly The Court doth therefore order that the said Ann Smith shall make acknowledgement of her fault in open Court wch was performed by the said Ann and likewise that she shall receive ten lashes upon her bare shoulders wch was remitted by the said Mr Presly And the Court doth further order that Robert Smith shall forthwith pay all the charges of Court x x"
Captions mutilated - ames Claughton agt - Pope	To next Court.
- - Trussell agt -ames Willis	This case is referred till the next Court in Chancery at Mr Trussell's motion.
- erseers of Jane Perrys will agt Tho Wilsford	Whereas it doth appear unto the Court that Thomas Wilsford doth owe unto the estate of the Widdow Perry deceased 960 lb of tobo and caske by Bill the Court doth therefore order that the said Wilsford shall forthwith make payment of the said debt with charges of Court unto Ralph Horsly x x "
John Haynie agt Tho Hailes admr Robt Honiborne	Hailes, admr of Robert Honnibourne decd ordered to pay 300 lb tobo to Haynie

Order Book #2. November 25th 1652. page 5.

Mr John Hallowes
agt
ffrancis Gray

Case referred to next Court in Mr Hallowes absence.

Hercules Bridges
to keep an
Ordinary

"The Court doth order that Hercules Bridges shall have License and Authority from this Court to Keepe an Ordinary till such time as he can procure a License from the Govnr and Counsell at James Citty"

Note: Puritans or no Puritans, the honorable Commissioners had to have a drink and have it then. So much for license. As for authority there is no indication of any weakness in the dispenser's name.   B.F.

Tho Hailes Quietus
est upon Robert
Honnibournes estate

"Whereas Thomas Hailes Administrator of Robert Honibourne hath given in an Inventory upon oath unto this Court And hath also passed his Accot upon the estate of the said Honnibourne By wch Accot it appeareth that the Administrator hath paid and laid out more than the decds estate would amount unto by the sum of ninety seaven pounds of tobaco The Court doth therefore order that the said Hales shall have a Quietus est"

ffrancis Gray
agt
Tho Knight

Referred to next Court in Knight's absence.

Mr ffran Clay
agt
Rich Span

Case referred to next Court.

Order Book #2. November 25th 1652. page 6.

Thomas Hailes
agt
Edward Hudsons

Entry mutilated. "Whereas it doth appear unto the Court by the deposition of James Willis and by the oath of Thomas Hailes that Edward Hudson doth owe unto the said Hailes 150 lb of tobo and that the said Hudson secretly departed this County without satisfying the said - - The Court doth therefore that the said Hailes - - have an attachment agt the estate of the said Hudson - - ever he can find any (after John Powell is - - his - - for the payment of the said debt with charges of Court"

Tho Roger
agt
Wm ffreake

Referred to next Court.

Order Book #2. 25th November 1652. page 6.

Mr Pope Attur - - Mr Hayward	Entry mutilated. "Whereas Mr Nathaniel Pope did introduce in Court a - - Atturney made by Mr Nicholas Hayward unto Richard - - his servant now

deceased as also a - - by the said Mr Hayward Directed to the said Mr Pope and likewise an Assignment from the said Nicholas of his - - of Atturney and the testimony and oath of Samuel Matthews had And desires the opinion of the Court whether an Acquittance given by the said Mr Pope for Tobacco received for the use of the said Mr Hayward was sufficient and legall by virtue of the writeings a foresaid receaved It was the opinion of the Court that Mr Popes acquittance for the Tobacco received for the account of the said Mr Hayward was sufficient and legall and doth discharge the - - that pay the tobaco sufficiently"

Mr Tho Speke agt Hen Barnes his estate	The Court orders payment of corn and tobo. to Mr Speke from estate of Barnes.
John Gundey agt Gabriel Odyer	Case referred to next Court in Odyer's absence.
Mr Speke Adm'r of Mr Edw Tempest	"The Court doth order that Mr Thomas Speke shall have a Commission of Administration granted of the estate of Mr Edward Tempest deceased he putting in an Inventory and security to the Court."
John Haney agt James Claughton	"James Claughton came into this Court and acknowledged Judgemt for the paymt of 300 lb of tabaco and caske with charges of Court by the next Court unto John Haney and execution"
John ffoster agt John Howard	Howard ordered to pay Foster 60 lb. of tobo. and Court charges.
Mr Turney agt Mr Trussell	Referred to next Court.
- - Smith and - Wilsford agt John Danby	"Whereas it was ordered the last that the Sherr and Clerke should pay unto John Danby 225 lb Tobo x x in satisfaction of a Bill wch Edward Hudson did enter into unto the said Danby for the paymt of 670 lb of tobo and caske The Court doth therefore order

that no execution shall issue out agt the said Sherr and Clerke till the said Danby doe assigne the said Bill over to the said Sherr and Clerke"

Order Book #2. 25th November 1652. page 6.

Capt Gyles Brent Admr of Mr John Rookewood decd	The Court orders that "Capt Giles Brent Esq" have com. of Admr. of Est. of Mr John Rookewood, decd. "always premised that if a greater creditor - - - administration the next Court then this order to be void"
Ralph Horsley Attur of Myles Cooke agt Arthur Branch	Branch owing Cooke 2280 lb tobo is ordered to pay, but Cooke must show that payment has been made to Branch for 100 lb. of sugar at 7 lb of tobo. per lb.
Barbary Dennis Admrx of Jno Dennis	Barbary Dennis, widow, to have com. of admr "of estate of John Dennis her husband decd "
John Haney attur of Matth Bassett agt Mr Trussell	Mr John Trussell owing Christopher Edwards 300 lb of tobo. the Court orders him to pay to John Haney, attorney of Matthew Bassett who is attorney of Edwards.

Order Book #2. 25th of November 1652. page 7.

John Haney Attur of Mr Wm Whitby agt Mr Trussell	Trussell owing Mr Wm Whitby, Administrator of Robert Alexander, 6 bbl. of corn, is ordered to pay Hayney, attorney for Whitby.
John Haney Attur of Jacob Simonson Haney agt Mr Trussell (sic)	"Whereas it doth appear unto the Court That Mr John Trussell doth owe unto Jacob Simonson Haney the sum of " 694 lb of tobo, Trussell is ordered to pay "to John Haney attur of the said Simonson Haney."
Mr Pope agt Tho Allens estate	The Court orders that Mr Nathaniel Pope have an attachment "against the estate of Thomas Allens decd in the hands of Thomas Youll for the satisfaction of ffive pounds fowerteene ounces of Beanes by Bill"

and 388 pounds of tabaco upon account. "and that notice be given to Tho Youlle."

Note: Evidently these beans were for seed, but even so, it is difficult for us in this day and time to realize their value. B.F.

Mr Speke his cert for Land	150 acres due for transportation of the following:
	    David Cristom
	    Wm Newberry
	    Mary Wooldridge

Order Book #2. November 25th 1652. page 7.

Mr Brodhurst his cert for Land	100 acres due for transportation into the colony the following:
	ffrancis Willis
	Patrick Potts

Collectors nominated — "The Court doth nominate and appoint Mr Walter Brodhurst to be Collector for Nominy and Appomattacly Tho Wilsford to be Collector for Enocomac and Cherrypoint to Matthew Rhodens and Mr Sam Smith to be Collector from Mr Cotansons downward to collect and gather the - - for this pressent year coming 085 - - (85 lb of tobacco per poll) As also for the Arrears of the last yeare Giving them full power and authority to d--eme in case of nonpaymt According to Act of Assembly

        Mr Brodhursts limitts hath   168 persons
        Tho Wilsfords Limitts hath   078
        Mr Smiths Limitts hath   144

                                       390

Note: From this I would estimate the population of Northumberland Co. to be about 1500, certainly not more than 2000 at the outside. B.F.

Robert Wyard agt Mr Rosier	This name is prob Wyatt. "This case is referred to the heareing and determination of Mr Speke Mr Pope Mr Hallowes and Mr Brodhurst"
Corbet Podle agt Mr Rosier	"This cause is referred to the same Com'rs for the determination thereof"
John Gresham agt Capt Brent	"This case is referred till the next second Court after this"
ffrancis Gray Guardian to Wm Buteler	"The Court doth order that ffrancis Gray shall be Guardian to Wm Buteler till he be of age and to keepe the cattle and their increase that shall belong unto him till he shall be one and twenty years of age The said Gray putting in security for the same and giving in an Accot of the female increase according to Act of Assembly in that case provided"
Colonel John Mottrom agt John Haney	Case referred to next Court.

Order Book #2. November 25th 1652. page 7.

Tho Coggin
agt
Jo Gresham

"Those whose names are underwritten being on a Jury in a case depending between Tho Coggin pltiff and John Gresham Defendt doe find by sufficient proof that as the Defendt did verbally bargain with the Pltiffe for a Cowe soe the Pltiffe did return the Cowe again as it appears by oath from his own acknowledgement unto the Defent And the Defendt never received nor the Pltiffe lawfully tendered any satisfaction for the said Cowe soe that we find it to be nothing but verball discourse we do therefore Award that the Defendt shall take into his possession the said Cowe with her increase since that the Pltiffe posessed her And likewise wee doe Award the Pltiffe to pay Court charges "

    Wm Thomas   Ralph Horsley   Wm Willdey
    Hugh Lee   Daniel Meels   Edm Brent
    Geo Mason   Matth Rhoden   Arthur Branch
    ffran Gray   John ffoster   John Bennett

Note: This jury made a discovery that applies to much of the hullabaloo in this old world-that it "be nothing but verball discourse."   B.F.

Wm Reynolds
agt
Tho Hawkins

"Whereas by bond given und'r the hand of Tho Hawkins it appears that the said Hawkins sold a man servant unto Wm Reynolds for the tearme of five years it being for longer time than the said Hawkins had - - power to dispose or the said servt right to serve as by Order of Court hath plainly appeared Wee do therefore with full consent allott that the said Hawkins shall performe and put into Wm Reynolds - - the opperacon of the fower yeares and as sufficient and able hand as that servant now in his custody is whether he live or dye so performe the compleate time of service as from bond from Hawkins is due unto the said Reynolds And wee do Allott Mr Hawkins to pay Court charges unto wch we have sett our hands "

    Wm Thomas   Matth Rhoden   Matt Coles
    Edw Thompson   Geo Berry   Wm Botts
    Charles Ashton   Rich Span   Corbet Podle
    ffra Gray   Herc Bridges   Ralph Horsley

Note: Yes-but-who was attending to Hercules' important business while he was on the jury ? B.F.

Mr John Trussell
agt
Gershon Cromwell

"The 27th of Novem 1652"
"Whereas it appeareth unto Mr Wm Presly that there is due to Mr John Trussell the sum of 104 lb of Tobo by the ack of Gershon Cromwell wherefore the said Mr Presly doth Order that the said Cromwell shall make present pay of the said debt or els execution"

Order Book #2. 25th November 1652. page 8.

Concerning Indians

" 25 November
Whereas divers of the Inhabitants of this County doe imploy Indians with guns and powder and shott very frequently and usually to the great danger of a Massacre The Court doth think fitt to declare and publish unto the whole county that if any person or persons what so ever shall within ten days after the date hereof deliver either gun powder or shott to any Indian under what pretence so ever shall be proceeded with all according to Act of Assembly in that case provided And that all maner of persons that have any guns out amongst the Indians after publication hereof shall get them in with all convenient speede And that no persons whatsoever imploy any Indian at all nor supply them with powder and shott "

Order Book #2. 20th January 1652/3. page 8.

"At a Court held for the County of Northumberland the 20th January 1652"

Present   Collo Jno Mottrom   Mr Wm Presly
             Lief Col Geo ffletcher   Mr John Hallowes
             Mr Thomas Speke   Mr Walter Brodhurst
             Mr John Trussell   Mr Sam Smith
                  Mr Nicho Morris

ffrances Symons
agt
Mr Rich Turney

Referred to next Court.

John Bennett
his cert for Land

"According to sufficient proofs made before this Court there is due to John Bennett Carpenter fifty acres of Land for transportation of Wm Spense into this colony"

Hugh ffouch
agt
Charles Williams
estate

Certain corn and tobacco awarded Fouch "for satisfaction of six months dyett the said Wms had with the said ffouch". 270 lb. tobo. to be paid Mr Tho Speke for debt of Charles Williams.

Corbet Podle
agt
- - Billingsby

"Whereas it doth appear unto the Court that Majr John Billingsby Executor of the Last will and Testament of Mr Robert Atkinson deceased doth owe unto Corbet Podle" 5000 lb of tobo. Billingsby ordered to pay out of the estate of Atkinson "allways provided that what goods or bedding the said Podle hath in his possession of the said deceased shall be delivered x x the said Majr Billingsby."

Order Book #2. 20th January 1652/3. page 8.

A Caveat agt Wm Cocke Ad'con	Let no Administration of the estate of William Cocke, deceased, be granted till Colonel John Mottrom be secured for the paymt of 6000 lb. of tobo x x .
John Gundry agt Gabriel Odger	The verdict of the Jury is not to be recorded and entered till one year be expired by consent of the attorneys of both sides.
Henry Brooks agt Majr Billingsby	Major Billingsby, executor of Mr. Robert Atkinson ordered to pay Brooks 200 lb. tobo. for coming to Court to appear as a witness in the proving of Atkinson's will.

Tho Wilsford agt John Davies — Whereas Thos Wilsford has pd 1000 lb. of tobo. to Wm. Thomas for damages in a case betw John Davies and Wm. Thomas "and whereas there doth now appear unto the Court that there was sinister and underhand dealing in the business by the said Davies The Court in Chancery doth therefore Decree and order that the said Jo Davies shall make present paymt of the said 1000 lb Tobo and Caske unto the said Wilsford with all charges of Court x x "

A ffree Schoole to be erected	"The Court doth allowe and approve of Mr Lees petcion concerning a free school to be set up "
Tho Saffell agt John Dodman	Referred to next Court.
Tho Hawkins agt Hen Cartwright	Cartwright came into Court and ack. a Judgmt of 250 lb of tobo to Hawkins.

Order Book #2. January 20th 1652/3. page 9.

Tho Hawkins agt Rich White	Referred to next Court in White's absence.
Wm Reynolds agt Tho Hawkins	Thos Hawkins having subpona'd Wm Reynolds to this Court as a witness agt Rich White Hawkins ordered to pay Reynolds 50 lb tobo for his charges with also charges of Court.
John Paine agt Tho Bassett	Bassett having subpoenaed Paine to Court as witness to prove will of "Mr Bolton decd" , the Court order Bassett to pay Paine 50 lb tobo for his charges.

Order Book #2.   20th January 1652/3.   Page 9.

George Day Adm'r of Mr Lonedons estate	The Court orders com. of admr. be granted Geo Day of the estate of Mr William Lonedon, decd., he putting in inventory and security.
Mr Robert Wyard agt George Day	Whereas George Day, Admr. of Mr Lonedon subpona'd Robert Wyard as witness, the Court orders Day to pay Wyard 50 lb. tobo for his charges.
Mr Trussell agt Walter Pakes	Pakes acks. Judgmt. 900 lb tobo to Mr. Jno Trussell
John Myles agt Walter Pakes	Case referred to next Court. Pakes ordered to put in security for his then appearance "before he depart the Court."
Mr Tho Speke agt John Aires	Aires owing 449 lb. tobo. to Edward Tempest, decd., the Court orders payment forthwith to Mr Thomas Speke, Admr. of Tempest.
Mr Pope agt Tho Allens estate	The estate of Thomas Allen, deceased, owing Mr Nathaniel Pope two pounds of beans, the Court orders that Thomas Youll make payment from the estate.

Note: While working in the Archives Department, one of the genealogists came to me and said "Mr. Fleet, you laugh at these people's ancestors. you must not do that. They do not like it." Now a good many of these early Virginians are my ancestors as well, so I will laugh if I want to. But not Mr. Nathaniel Pope, so far as I know. There is not the slightest suggestion of mirth in making the foregoing abstract. B.F.

Mr Hugh Lee agt Walter Pakes	"Whereas Mr Hugh Lee did petition the Court and made it appear that he hath a Bill out for the payment of seaven Barrells of Indian Corne and Eight hundred weight of Porke to be paid to John

Hamond and the said Hamond did assign the said Bill over to Walter Pakes and the said Lee hath paid 2800 lb. of tobaco and caske in satisfaction of the said Bill to Mr Robert Pitt mercht and half of the said 2800 lb of tobaco and caske being the said Hamonds owne pre'y Debt and whereas yet the said Lee cannot get in the said Bill and whereas the said Walter Pakes did sweare upon his Corporall oath that he hath none of the said Bill in his deposition but that the said Bill is lost for anything he knows and that he hath not seene the Bill this Two yeares The Court doth order that if ever the Bill be found againe or come to the hands of the said Walter Pakes that he deliver the same to the said Mr Lee or his assignes"

Note: It looks as though the said Mr Pakes were just a little bored at the 'said Mr Lee's business ability. B.F.

Order Book #2.   20th January 1652/3.   Page 9.

Mr Lloyd
agt
Mr Turney

Referred to next Court.

Mr Walter Brodhurst
agt
Mr Pope

"The Court doth order that Mr Nathaniel Pope Atturney of Mr Nicholas Hayward of London mercht shall out of the said Mr Haywards estate make x x paymt of 2000 lb of tobo and Caske unto Mr Walter Brodhurst for being Generall Atturney of the said Mr Hayward in the yeare 1651 x x "

Mr Wm Presly
agt
Jeremy Cooper

"Whereas Jeremy Cooper hath sumoned or Arrested Mr Wm Presly to this Court and the said Cooper doth not declare agt him neither by himself nor his atturney The Court doth therefore order that the said Cooper shal be nonsuited and pay unto the said Mr Presly 50 pounds of tobacco forthwith for a nonsuit with charges of Court x x"

Wm Cornish
agt
Jeremy Cooper

"Whereas Jeremy Cooper hath arrested Wm Cornish" and not appearing against him, is nonsuited and ordered to pay Cornish 50 lb. tobo and Court charges

Order Book # 2.   20th January 1652/3.   page 10.

Mr Turney
agt
Mr Trussell

Referred to next Court.

Mr Clay
agt
Rich Span

Referred to next Court.

Mr Hallowes
agt
Geo Day

Whereas Mr Wm Lonedon decd., owed Mr John Hallowes 500 lb of tobo., the Court orders Day, Admr. of Mr Lonedon to pay.

ffrancis Gray
agt
Tho Knight

Referred to next Court.

Order Book #2. 20th January 1652/3. page 10.

Mr Hallowes agt Tho Knight	Knight owing Hallowes 1440 lb of tobo "and the said Knight hath been arrested and doth not appear by himself nor atturney the Court orders x x that if the said Knight do not appear the next Court and Answere the suite then Ordr shall pass agt Mr Rosier Knights security"
Hen Wicher agt Martine Cole	"Whereas Martine Cole hath arrested Hen Wisher to this Court and the said Cole doth not declare agt him" the Court orders Cole nonsuited and that he pay Wicher 50 lb. tobo. and also Court costs.
Appraisers of Mr Lonedons esta	Tho Youll and John Myles appointed appraisers of the estate of Mr. Wm London (sis).
Collo Mottrom Admr of Wm Cooke estate	Court order that Col. John Mottrom have com. of Admr. of estate of Wm Cooke, decd., and that he first pay himself 6000 lb. of tobo. due by bills.
John Gresham agt Mr Morris	Referred to next Court in Gresham's absence.
John Waddy agt Colo Mottrom	The Court orders Col. John Mottrom, Admr. of est. of Wm Cocke to pay to John Waddy 600 lb of tobo. from the estate of the deceased "for funerall charges and attendance of the decd in the time of his sickness. "
Mr Tulney (sic) agt Ralph Ashton	Referred to next Court.
Edward Coles Surveyor	"The Court doth ordr and appoint Edward Coles to be Surveyor for this yeare for this County for the marking out of High-wayes "

Note: So here is a Highway Engineer in 1653. B.F.

Order Book #2.   January 20th 1652/3   page 10.

James Claughton "Whereas there was a difference depending between
agt   James Claughton pltf and Mr Nathaniel Pope deft
Mr Pope   concerning a bill of Three Cowes woe finde the Bill
                 not be Authenticke the said Pope alleadging non est
factum and the said Claughton being not able to make proofs thereof
wee do therefore awarde the said Pope to be cleere of the aforesaid
Bill and that the said Claughton ought to pay the Charges of the Court"

    Wn Thomas   Ralph Horsly   Matth Rhodon
    Daniel Meels   Hen Rayner   John Haney
    Hen Brooke   Rch fflynt   Hen Rocke
    Hen Mosely   Tho Sheapard   Jacob Cotancean

Rich fflynt   "Whereas there is a difference depending betweene
agt   Rich fflynt pltiffe and Sarah the wife of Andrew
Sarah Bowyer   Bowyer Defent concerning a Defamacon wch upon the
                 request of the said Sarah Bowyer was referred to
a Jury Wee whose names are underwritten can find no sufficient proofs
that the said Bowyers wife ever Defamed the said Richard fflynt his
wife or Mother. But it seemed rather as by proofs it is evident more
- - of malice then evidenced evidenced being grounded upon a former
differance betweene Cyprian Bishopp and Bowyers wife wee doe therefore
Awarde that the said fflynt shall pay all the charges of Court and make
good all such Damages as Sarah Bowyer shall make appear to the Court
and wee doe further Awarde that Rich fflynt pay to the Clerke of the
Court 30 pounds of tobaco for his drawing up of this Verdict In wittnes
whereof wee have and - - set our hands the 20th of Jann 1652 x x "

    Wm Thomas   Wm Reynolds   Wm ffreake
    Jo Haney   Tho Sheapard   James Claughton
    Ro Wyard   Sim Richardson   John Waddy
    Jo Myles   ffran Gray   Tho Blagg

Sarah Bowyer   Flynt ordered by the Court to pay Sarah Bowyer
agt   250 lb. tobo. damages.
Rich fflynt

Order Book #2.   20th January 1652/3.   page 11.

Tho Blagg   According to sufficient proofs there is due to
his cert for   Thos Blagg 100 acres for transportation of himself
Land   and Judith Spencer into the colony.

Mr Cotanreane   "Whereas there was several differences in a case
agt   depending in Northumberland Court between Mr Jacob
Mr Tulney   Cotanreane and Mr Richard Tulney and the Com'rs of
                the said Court with the consent of the said
Cotanreane and Tulney transmitted their cause to be made and end of by
me Now know yee that upon examination of their accounts I find the said

Order Book #2. 20th January 1652/3. page 11

Turney to be indebted unto Mr Jacob Cotanreane in the - - some and quanity of 875 lbs of good merchantable tobaco and caske with 100 lb. of porke to be paid at Demands And I do further Ordor that the said partics shall give to each other discharges and each other - - show charges expended in the sute Witnos my hand the 29th of Novem 1652
                                               John Mottrom
20 Jane 1652 Recorded this order   "

Order Book #2. 10th March 1652/3. page 11.

"Att a Court held for the County of Northumberland the 10th day of March 1652 "
Present   Colonel John Mottrom   )
          Mr Thomas Speke   )   Mr John Hallowes
          Mr John Trussell   )
          Maj'r Tho Baldridge   )   Com'rs

Mr Pope Admr of   "The Court doth ord'r that a Commission of Admr shal
Jon Cooke   be granted to Mr Nathaniel Pope of the estate of
Cum   John Cooke deceased Cum Testamento - -annexo (sic)
   to   The will being proved now by Abraham Jerman a witnes
Testam annexo   to the said will x x "

Mr Hallowes   "Whereas it doth appear unto the Court that Wm
agt   Cooke doth - - unto Mr John Hallows for the account
Colo Mottrom Admr   of Capt Henry ffleete the sum of 1750 pounds of
of Wm Cooke   tobaco and caske by Bill The Court doth order that
                      Colonel John Mottrom Administrator of the said
Cooke shall out of the deceaseds estate make paymt of the said debt
unto the said Mr Hallowes (after the Accot - - John Waddy are satisfyed
- - debts) x x "

Mr Hallowes   John Cooke owing to Mr John Hallowes assignee of
agt   John Danby and Mr - - West, 902 lb. of tobo., the
Mr Pope Admr of   Court orders Mr. Pope to pay from the deceaseds
John Cooke   estate.

Mrs Marga Brent   Wm Cooke owing Mrs Margaret Brent 311 lb tobo, Col
agt   Mottrom is ordered to pay"Capt Gyles Brent Esq.,
Colo Mottrom   atturney of the said Mrs Margaret Brent"
Admr Wm Cooke

Order Book #2. 10th of March 1652/3. page 11.

Wm Hardich agt Mr Hallowes	The Court orders Mr John Hallowes to pay 300 lb. tobo. to William Hardich "for the wrong he hath done unto the said Hardich his Boate"

Mr Hallowes   The Court orders that Mr John Hallowes have an
agt   attachment agt Mr Chichester's estate "for the
Mr Chichester   satisfaction of 300 pounds of tobaco and caske
                     wch the said Mr Hallowes was ordered by this Court
to pay unto William Hardich for the wrong done to the said Hardich his
Boate wth charges of Court (wch said wrong was done to the Boate by the
said Mr Chichester) "

Mary Keene
her cert for Land
	"According to sufficient proofs made before this Court there is due to Mary Keene 200 acres of Land for the transportation of these persons following into this colony Vizt:
	    Tho Keene Wm Keene &
	    Her Selfe Susan Keene "

Capt Cornewaleys agt Mr Pope Admr John Cooke	Referred to next Court.
Mr Hallowes agt Mr Rosier	"The Court doth order that Mr John Rosier Clerk shall within ten days make payment of 1740 pounds of tobaco and caske unto Mr John Hallowes with charges of Court as security for Tho Knight according to an order of the last Court and execution"
Capt Giles Brent Esq agt Hugh Lee	"Whereas Capt Brent hath arrested Hugh Lee to this Court The Court doth adjudge that the case hath formerly been tryed and is ended"

page 12.

Capt Cornewalyes agt Mr Speke Admr of Mr Tempest	Mr Edward Tempest owing Capt Thomas Cornewalyes, Attorney of Thos Matthews, 20 pounds sterling (by Mr Speke's confession), Speke is ordered to pay 4000 lb. tobo. and cask from the deceased's estate in lieu of the 20 pounds sterling.

page 12

Mr Hallowes agt Mr Speke Admr of Mr Tempest.	Edward Tempest owing Mr John Hallowes assignee of Capt. Wm Michell, 500 lb. of tobo. Speke is ordered to pay from the deceased's estate.

Order Book #2. 10th March 1652/3. page 12.

Corbet Podle
agt
Mr Turney

Referred to next Court in Mr Turney's absence.

Mr Cotancean
freed from Levies

"Whereas Mr Jacob Cotancean did make it appeare unto the Court that he is about 67 yeares of age Therefore the Court doth order that he shall not hereafter be putt into the list for the paymt of County and Country Levies"

ffrancis Simons
agt
Mr Turney

Referred to next Court.

Mr Turney
agt
Mr Jacob Cotanceawe

Referred to next Court.

John Hall
his cert for
Land

"According to sufficient proofs made before this Court there is due to John Hull 400 acres of Land for the transportation of these persons following into this Colony Vizt:
    John Ser-en (Sermen, Scriver ? ?)
    Tho Mecham
    Cha Parker
    Walt Moore
    Ann ffeild
    Judith Layton (or Juduh Layton)
    Samu: Dunn
    Marge Clever (or Marye Cluer)
Written in here in a different hand, evidently added much later is: "March the 21 1684/5 The five first were assigned over to Richd Smyth per Richd Hull - -es - of 7th sd- - " This entry is so faded that it is illegible here.

Mr Hallowes to
-treme for Mr
Sedgravs fees

"Whereas Mr Robert Sedgrave hath divers fees oweing him as Sherriffe and Clerke of this County Court and divers persons make refusall of paymt thereof the Court doth therefore order that the persons who are indebted to him for fees shall make pmt thereof to Mr John Hallowes Administrator of the said Mr Sedgrave or else for default of paymt it shall be lawfull for the said Mr Hallowes to Distreme "

Order Book #2.   10th March 1652/3.   page 12.

Mr Trussell agt Robert Sharps estate	Order that Mr John Trussell have attachment against the estate of Robt. Sharpe for 450 lb. tobo.
John Gresham agt Capt Brent Esq	The Court orders that the Jury be dismissed and the case referred to next Court for Simon Richardson's further deposition.
Henry Wicher agt Martin Cole	Case referred to next Court.
Capt. Brent, Attur of Mrs Marga Brent agt Jno Gresham	Case referred to next Court.
Majr Baldridge killing a wolf	The Court orders Major Tho. Baldridge to have 100 lb. tobo. for killing a wolf.
Henry Wicher agt Martin Cole	The Court orders that Wicher be nonsuited in case against Cole.

Order Book #2.   20th May 1653.   page 12.

"Att a Court held for the County of Northumberland the 20th day of May 1653"
Prest.   Colonel John Mottrom
               Mr John Trussell
               Mr Walter Brodhurst
               Mr Nicho Morris   Comrs.

John Cetanceam agt Mr Turney	Whereas Mr Richard Turney owes John Cetanceam 640 lb. tobo., the Court orders payment to Corbet Podle, assignee of Cetanceam.
John Gresham agt Capt Brent	"Whereas John Gresham Attur of John Abbott has arrested Capt Gyles Brent Esq for 3000 lb of tobaco it appears by oath of Simon Richardson and the deposition of John Lee " - the account ordered settled.

Order Book #2. 20th May 1653. page 13.

Mrs Marga Brent agt John Gresham Attur of Jo Abbott	John Abbott owing to Leonard Calvert Esq., 1250 lb tobo. the Court orders that John Gresham Admr of Abbott pay to Capt. Giles Brent, Attorney of Mrs Margaret Brent, Admx of the said Mr. Calvert by the next Court.
ffran Simons agt Mr Turney	Richard Turney owing ffrancis Simons 300 lb. tobo. ordered to pay within ten days.
Clement Corbell his cert for Land	"According to x proofs made x Clement Corbell has due him 550 acres of Land for transporting the following into the colony" 　　Himselfe　　　　　　　Samuel Nicholls 　　Angell his wife　　　　ffranc Jones 　　Gabriell Corbell　　　Henry Sentenee 　　John Corbell　　　　　James Peirce 　　Anne Corbell　　　　　Marga Barrow 　　Angell Corbell
Ann Compton agt Colo Mottrom Admr of Wm Cocke	Wm. Cocke owing Ann Compton 390 lb tobo., the Court orders Col. Jno. Mottrom, Admr., to pay.
John Danby agt Mr Sampson Calvert	Case referred to next Court.
Tho Orlye his cert for Land	"According to sufficient proofs made before this Court there is due to Thomas Orlye one hundred acres for his own transportation twice into this colony"

Note: This name may, of course, be Thomas Hawley. B.F.

"According to the power and authority given to the Com'rs of this County by Act of Assembly The Court doth limitt and bound the parishes within the said County of Northumberland as followeth Vizt:

Chickacone Parish bounded Nominye Parish	Chichacone parish from Wicocomacoe Island inclusively to John Powells inclusively Nominy parish from John Powells exclusively all Nominy and Appomattachy and soe upwards
Great Wicocomocoe Parish	Great Wicocomocoe parish from the Dividing Creeke to Mr Samu: Smiths where he now liveth inclusively and all the inhabitants on the Southward side of Little Wicocomocoe Creeke "
Henry Raynor his cert for Land	According to sufficient proofs, etc., 100 acres due for transportation of these into the colony: 　　Archibald Reade 　　Thomas Watson.

Order Book #2. 20th May 1653. page 13.

Gyles Tavenor
agt
Hercules Bridges

Hercules Bridges owing Gyles Tavernor 960 lb. tobo., the Court orders that if "Phillip Silvester who is security for the said Bridges doe not bring forth the said Bridges to the next that then Ord'r to pass agt the said Baile for the paymt of the said debt unto Richard Holden Atturney of the said Tavernor with forbearance and Charges of Court also execution"

Note: Now the honorable Commissioners knew very well that Hercules did not have time to step over to the Court House. And who was this Gyles anyway and why should he be allowed to upset the social system of Northumberland County for the sake of his darned old tobacco ? B.F.

John Johnson
exempted
from Levies

John Johnson to be exempt from paying County and Country levies "in respect of his lameness and inability to worke wch was contracted in the service of the Country in the last Massacre"

Note: Now here is an ancestor that someone may well be proud of. We cannot but wonder how many a hardy hero may be among these unknown names. B.F.

Tho Rodger
agt
Wm ffreake

Freake owing Rodger 1240 lb. tobo. "The Court doth order that if the Sheriffe do not bring forth the body of the said ffreake unto the next Court then ord'r to pass agt the sheriffe for his paymt of the said debt x x "

Note: Please note the personal responsibility of the sheriff in such cases. B.F.

Thomas Rice
agt
Corbet Podle

Case referred to next Court.

John Davies
agt
Wm Thomas

Thomas owing Davies 200 lb. pork and 170 lb tobo., ordered to pay within ten days.

Robert Butt
agt
John Dedman

Dedman owing Butt 524 lb. tobo. "the Court orders that the Sheriffe in default in not taking Baile shall within ten days make paymt of said debt unto Wm Thomas Atturney of Tho G- - assignee of the said Butts x x".

Order Book #2. 20th of May 1653. page 14.

Mr Sam Smith
agt
John Dedman

"Whereas the Court did order that the Sheriff should within ten days make paymt of 524 lb. tobo. x unto Wm Thomas Atturney of Thomas Gassall assignee of Robert Butt in default of not taking Baile of John Dedman" the Court now orders that Dedman makes paymt within ten days.

Capt Hackett
agt
Hugh Lee'

Case referred to next Court.

27

Note: We have all of us heard of the Barnes-Ashton case. Often the suggestion is worse than the fact. So here it is in complete detail.
B. F.

Order Book #2. 20th May 1653. page 14.

John Barnes
agt
Mr Ashton

"Whereas wee whose names are underwritten were impanelled on a Jury betweene John Barnes Pltiffe and Mr Charles Ashton Defendt concerning an aspercon case upon the said Barnes by the said Mr Ashton In saying that the said Barnes had gott his maide servant deceased with Childe and had given her the pox All wch the said Barnes hath proved by the oathes of three famous witnesses and the said Mr Ashton cannot defend by any legall and pertinent evidence wee doe therefore Awarde that the said Mr Ashton shall have his choice either to pay to the said Barnes on the 10th day of Novem next the sume of Three hundred and fifty pounds of good Tobco in Caske for the reparacon of the said Barnes his Creditt or - - (page mutilated) Aske him forgivenes in open Court with the paymt of all Court Charges expended in this suite As witnes our hands the 20th of May 1653

    John Haynie   Ralph Horsley   Rich White
    John Grosham   Jon Bennett   David Spiller
    Matth Rhodon   Robt Bradshaw   Abrah Byram
    James Willis   Tho Orley   Hen Moseley "

Phebe Kent
her Depo

"Phebe Kent aged 22 yeares or thereabouts being sworne and examined saith That this Depont did help to bury the servant maide of Mr Charles Ashton and saw her dead body to be a cleare Coarse and free from the pox to the best of this Depon'ts knowledge And further saith not Phebe Kent her marke Jurat in Curt "

Hugh Lee
his Depo

"Hugh Lee aged 44 yeares or thereabouts being sworne and examined saith That about the middle of Novem last Mr Charles Ashton came to my house and in the presence of Mrs Rocke and my wife he told me that John Barnes had given his maide the pox and had begott her with Childe and there was something stirred in her belly and further saith not Hugh Lee Jurat in Cur"

Hannah Lee
her Depo

"Hannah Lee aged 37 yeares or thereabouts being sworne and examined saith That about the middle of Novem last Mr Charles Ashton came to my house and told me in the presence of my husband and Mrs Rocke That John Barnes had given his maide the pox and had begott her with Childe and that she had something stired in her belly At another time the maide came hither and I asked whether John Barnes had promised to marry her and persuaded her to runaway that he might make the easier composicon for her And she answeared never and wished the ground might open and she sinke in if ever Barnes did say any such thing to her but she said that she was a poore servant and she must und'rgoe what her Mr and Mrs would report And further saith not Hannah Lee her marke Jurat in Cur "

Order Book #2. 20th May 1653. page 14.

Katherine Rocke
her Depo

"Katherine Rocke aged 21 yeares or thereabouts sworne saith That what Hannah Lee hath declared as abovsaid is the whole truth to the best of her knowledge Katherine Rocke Jurat in Cur "

Mr Trussell
his Depo

"The Deposicon of John Trussell aged 50 yeares or thereabouts this 20th day of May 1653 being examined saith That about ten days before Mr Ashton his servant maide died the wife of the said Mr Ashton came to my house and earnestly desired me this Depont to goe with her to her house to speake with her husband and I coming to his said house Mr Ashton told me that his maide was very sicke and she often complained of John Barnes that he the said Barnes was the cause of her sicknes He the said Mr Ashton desired me to see her and heare what she would say concerning John Barnes and I goeing into the roome where she lay She the said servant told me that John Barnes often perswaded her to run away from her master and when she was gone he would lay her and then may be he should have her cheape by whose perswasions she often had soe done ffurther she told me that he the said Barnes had promised her marriage and affirmde it with many oathes and serious professacons and he had by his protestacons the use of her body and did lye with her three or fower severall times she nominating both the dayes and places with many other the like words she made relacon of concerning him the said John Barnes wch now this Depont canot well call to remembrance soe much I this Depont can say and no more   John Trussell "

Note: Yes, it was unfortunate that the Judge could not remember more—as if this were not too much as it was. B.F.

Walter Weekes
his Depo

"Walter Weekes aged 37 yeares or thereabouts Deposeth on oath that comeing to Mr Ashtons when his made was sicke was requested by the maide to speake to John Barnes to come to her and she said she would prove more to Barnes face then ever she spake already to her Mrs wch this Depont heard Mrs Ashton say that the maide related that John Barnes had given her the pox ffurther saith that doeing that message to Barnes Mr Lee replyed that he should not goe to her but if he had done her wrong let the law right her   Walter Weekes Jurat in Cur "

Note: Now if so much came out in Court, you can well imagine the idle gossip that was passed from group to group throughout the countryside regarding the very personal affairs of John Barnes. No wonder , that backed by his substantial friends the Lees, he struck back. And struck in the open right at the root of the evil.
    As unfortunate as this affair was in early Virginia, it is a mere nothing as compared with happenings of the same period in London, Dublin, Edinburgh—not to mention Paris and Rome.   B.F.

Order Book #2. 20th Sept. 1653. page 15.

"Att a Court held for the County of Northumberland the 20th of Septem 1653"

    Present   Colonel John Mottrom Esq
                Mr. John Trussell
                Mr Wm Presly
                Mr Nicho Morris   Com'rs

Tho Saffall exempted from Levies — "The Court doth order That Thomas Saffall shall (de future) be exempted from paymt of County Levies he being 69 yeares of age as he hath taken his oath before Mr Nicholas Morris"

John Standley his cert for goeing for England — "Whereas John Stanley hath affixed his name at the doore of the Court House for this County according to Act of Assembly concerning his goeing for England this next shipping The Court doth therefore order that he shall have a Cert to the Secretaryes Office at James Citty "

Wm Reynolds his cert for Land — According to sufficient proofs, etc., 100 acres are due Wm Reynolds for transportation into this colony of:
    Wm Linsey
    Tho Backster

John Powell agt Mr Joseph Maning — "Whereas x x by oaths of Robert Laud and Thomas Philpott x x also by a x x writing x x of Joseph Maning x x that Maning hired a sloop of John Powell x x the said sloope was never returned " The sloop now being of little worth by neglect, the Court orders Mr Charles Ashton to pay 1000 lb. tobo. out of that he owes to Manning.

Ralph Horsley agt Colo Mottrom Admr of Wm Cooke — Cooke having owed Horsley 640 lb tobo. Col. Mottrom, Admr. is ordered to pay.

Capt Tho Cornewaleys agt Mr Pope Admr of John Cooke — John Cooke owing to Daniel Clocker 350 lb. tobo., the Court orders Mr. Nathaniel Pope, Admr. of said Cooke to pay Capt. Thomas Cornewaleys, assignee of Clocker, by Nov. 10th next, from the estate.

Mr Pope his - - itus est upon Wm Cooks estate — Mr Nathaniel Pope, Admr. of the estate of John Cooke, decd., having rendered an account to the Court, it is ordered that he have a Quietus est.

Robert Laud his cert for Land — According to sufficient proofs, etc. 100 acres are due for transportation of following into the colony:
    ffrancis Berry
    Mary Dicks

Order Book #2. 20th Sept. 1653. page 15.

John Danby agt Mr Calvert	Mr. Sampson Calvert, Clerk, owing John Danby, assignee of Mr. Richard Turney 612 lb. tobo. ordered to pay by Nov. 20th.
Colo Mottrom his Quietus est upon Mr Suningberks estate	Whereas Col. John Mottrom, Admr of the estate of Mr fflorentino Suningberke has given to the Court an account, showing that he had paid out more than the estate amounted to by 1200 lb. tobo., order is given that he have his Quietus est.
Walter Weekes Constable	"The Court doth nominate and appoint Walter Weekes to be Constable for Chickacone this yeare and that he take his oath before a Com'r."
Tho Kedby Undr Sherriffe	"Tho Kedby was sworne Under Sherriffe for this County"

Order Book #2. 20th Sept. 1653. page 16.-this page badly stained and torn.

Mr Dod- - agt Mr Sampson	Case referred to next Court at Mr Dodson's motion.
James Macgregger agt Tho Hawkins	Hawkins owing McGregor 13 pair of shoes is ordered to pay.
Tho Hawkins agt James Macregger	McGregor owing Hawkins 1181 lb. tobo. is ordered to pay to William Thomas, Attorney for Hawkins by Nov. 20th.
Thomas Kedger agt Wm ffreake	Freake owing Kedger 350 lb. tobo. ordered to pay by Nov. 20th.
John Danby agt Mr Turney	Richard Turney acks. debt to John Danby of 400 lb. tobo. Will pay Nov. 20th.
Tho Hawkins agt John Bennet Seaman	Case referred to next Court.
Colonel Claybourne agt Mr -ewman	Part of page missing here.

Order Book #2. 20th Sept. 1653. page 16. This page stained and torn.

Tho Hawkins
agt
Rich White

"Richard White x x acknowledge before Mr Trussell and those in Court that he had x x Thomas Hawkins wrong in saying that the said Hawkins was a perjured fellow and the said White promiseth to pay charges of Court else execution Rich White his marke "

Wm Clapham Senr
agt
Mr fflynt

Richard fflynt owing Wm. Clapham, Sr., 1086 lb. tobo. ordered to pay Wm. Thomas, attorney for Clapham by Nov. 20th.

Mr. Lee
agt
John Danby

Danby owing Mr. Hugh Lee 605 lb. tobo and a barrel of corn, ordered to pay by Nov. 20th.

John Danby
agt
Mr Lee

"The Court doth order that Mr Hugh Lee shall pay all the - - of Corne due till the time of his making sale of Porke x unto John Danby and that he carry over the said Corne to Mary-Land by the 20th of Novem: next and if he call upon John Danby the said Danby doth promise to goe along with the said Lee to - - the said corne to the Secretary of Mary-Land and the said Danby will stand to the -ard of corne after the -der is made"

John Michael Attur
of Jacob Simonson
agt
Edward Hull

"The Court doth Ord'r that if Edward Hull doe not - - the next Court then ord'r to pass against his - - for the paymt of 508 lb. of Tobaco and Caske "

Capt Hacket
agt
Mr Lee

Referred to next Court at Mr. Lee's motion.

Rich Span
Constable
for Little Wicocomoco

"And was sworne in Court"

John Hulet
agt
Wm Thomas

"Wee whose names are hereund'r written being impannelled on a Jury in a case depending between John - - - William Thomas Defendt - - said John Hulet Three hun- - - Caske - -" page torn away.

    Hugh Lee   - - Span   Rich Turney
    Rich fflynt   John Ingram   Rich White
    John Sampson   Tho Sheapard   Ger Dodson
    Simon Richardson   Nath Hickman   John Chambers

Note: See depositions to follow. B.F.

Order Book #2. 20th September 1653. page 17.

Eliza Wood her Depo	"The Deposition of Elizabeth Wood aged 31 yeares or Thereabouts saith that she was frequently conversant with and about (part of page gone here) - - - - wife of John Hulet deceased and after her death did helpe to stripp and lay forth the said Hannah and ffound her a very cleare Coarse without any blemish or the least appearance of any abuse and was then with childe not having had any mischance before her death And further saith not Signed Elizabeth Wood "
Eliza Baker her Depo	"Elizabeth Baker aged 21 yeares or thereabouts deposeth the same verbatum Signum Elizabeth Baker her Dep Teste Tho Ballard Clic Cur " (sic)
John Hopper his depo	"John Hopper aged 25 yeares or thereabouts being sworne and examined saith That he this Depont being at Edward Coles heard Wm Thomas say to John Hulet that he had given Radford a note ond'r (sic) John Hulets hand to receave a Barrell and 3 pecks of Corne at Richard Gibbles the said Thomas asked if he was contented with it the said Hulet said yes if it were paid at Martin Coles And further saith not John Hopper his marke 20th Septem 1653 Jurat in Cur "
John Radfords Depo	"The Deposicon of John Radford saith That he tolde Wm Thomas that he was to have a Barrell of Corne of Wm Botts and the said Thomas answered that the Bachelers (sic) ordered me to charge it for them whereupon the said Thomas gave me a note to fetch the corne in his name at Richard Gribble house but the said Gribble denyed the delivery thereof untill he had a - - - - soe I returned the note unto Mr Thomas and he paid the Corne unto me soe I meeting with John Hulet I told him that I had a note from Mr Thomas for the Corne and he tolde me that it was well soe so he could have his Corne paid upon (page stained here) - - - - - John Radford Jurat Coram me Jo Mottrom "
Edward - - his Depo	Entry mutilated. Page torn and part missing. "- -d Coles sworne saith that he heard William - - tell John Hulet that he had changed his - - - - - Corne - - - - - me John Trussell "
John Hopper his Depo	"John Hopper aged 25 yeares or thereabouts being sworne and examined saith that he this Depont heard John Hulet say that he had a Copy of the Ord' that cleared him from the death of his wife And further saith not John Hopper his marke Jurat in Cur "

Order Book #2. 20th Sept. 1653. page 17. This page torn and part missing.

Tho Hopkins his Depo
"Thomas Hopkins aged 36 sworne and examined saith Septem - - 1653 Being at the house of Thomas Gaskins - - - - of a Cup of wyne John Hulet being in Company - - - an abuseing way rise up and said he must have cleres and further sitting downe rose up againe saying I must have blood before I goe to bed the said John Hulet rising up some words past betweene them the said John Hulet saying that Wm Thomas was a Cheater and that he would prove him a Cheater and that he went up and down the Country Cheating of folks whereupon words rise betwixt the said Hulet and Wm Thomas and Wm Thomas called the said Hulet Rogue and that he would prove it and that he was taxed for murthering of his wife and whereupon the said Hulet showed a peeee of pap'r that he was cleared Thomas Hopkins "

Tho Brewer his Depo
"Thomas Brewer testifying of the same onely the peece of pay (sic) he did not see The marke of Tho Brewer Jureatr Coram me Jo Mottrom"

Note: Something tells me that more than one cup of wyne was handed around at Mr. Gaskins delightful entertainment. We would assume, that in spite of the mutilated page that it was Mr. Thomas who wanted the blood, Mr. Hulet already having had some, thank you, the little peece of paper nevertheless to the contrary. While we would like to report Mr. Thomas to his descendants as a great merchant of early Northumberland, who traded up and down the bay, Mr. Hulet's remark spoils that.
B.F.

Order Book #2. 22nd Sept. 1653. page 17.

"At a Court held for the County of Northumberland at Colonel Mottroms house 22th of Septem 1653"
Present   Colonel Wm Claiborne Esq
             Colonel John Mottrom
             Mr John Trussell
             Mr Wm Presly

"The Court doth Ord'r that Colo Claiborne shall have an Attachm't agt the estate of Wm Porter decd for a debt of 300 lb. of Tobo and Cask due to the said Colo Claibourne with forbemnce"

Note: We cannot but admire the forbearance of the brave Colonel who sues a dead man and acts as a judge in the case. B.F.

34

Order Book #2. 21st November 1653. page 17.

"At a Court held for the County of Northumberland the 21st of Novem 1653"
Present   Colonel John Mottrom
                Mr John Trussell
                Mr Wm Presley
                Mr Nicho Morris   Com'rs

Colo Mottrom agt Phi- Ca- - Edward Henley   Entry mutilated. "This day came into the Court - - - - the payment of one - - - pounds of Tobo - - unto Colo Mottrom or his assignes with Charges of Court else execution Phillip Carpenter Edward Henley "

Order Book #2. 21st November 1653. page 18. This page badly mutilated and parts gone.

Collo M- - agt Phillip Carpenter   An agreement between Col. John Mottrom and Phillip Carpenter, in which Carpenter acknowledges the purchase of certain cattle and hogs from Mottrom and agrees to pay 2332 lb. tobo for them. Entry signed Phillip Carpenter.

Hugh Loe agt Peter Knight   This part of page mutilated and partly missing.

Colo Mottrom agt John E- -   ditto

Robert Sh-- - -   Ditto

Colo Mottrom agt John Walker   John Walker acks. a debt of 800 lb. tobo to Col. Mottrom. Signed John Walker his marke

John Haney his cert for Land   According to sufficient proofs, etc., there is due to Jno Haney 100 acres for the transportation of the following into the colony.
        David a Scotchman
        John Duglas

Note: These early clerks simply could not spell the Scottish names. We, with a superior air, wonder if he had any idea as to where John Douglas came from. B.F.

Order Book #2. 21st November 1653. page 18.

Richard Budd agt Mr Calvert Diff	Case referred to next Court at Mr. Calvert's motion.
Richard Budd Attur of - - - - -	This case referred to next Court at Mr Calvert's motion.
Tho Brewer agt Mr Calvert	"Whereas Mr Sampson Calvert hath arrested Tho Brewer unto this Court and hath no cause of Action", the Court orders Calvert to pay Brewer 50 lb. tobo. and to pay Court charges.
Tho Youell agt - - -	Illegible. Page mutilated and partly missing.
Tho Hawkins agt John Earle	ditto.
Mr Trussell agt Robert Sharpe	ditto.

Order Book #2. 21st November 1653. page 19.

Tho Hawkins agt Phillip Carpenter	Carpenter acks. Judgmt. 1094 lb. tobo.
Tho Hawkins agt Tho Hailes	Hailes acks. Judgmt. 927 lb. tobo.
Mr Hallowes agt Anth Linton	Linton acks. Judgmt. 1400 lb tobo.
Tho Hawkins agt Tho Sheapard	Sheapard owing Hawkins 533 lb. tobo. ordered to pay.

Order Book #2. November 21st 1653. page 19.

Joseph Wicks agt David Spiller	Spiller owing Wicks 200 lb. tobo. "for worke done by the said Wicks his servant for him the said Spiller by the testimony of Tho Brewer", Spiller is ordered to pay forthwith.
- - Maddox agt Phillip Carpenter	Carpenter acks. Judgmt. for 350 lb. tobo.
Tho Hawkins agt Hen Rooke	Rooke acks. Judgmt for 1500 lb tobo due Hawkins.
Mr Speke agt Hugh ffouch	Fouch owing Speke 1729 lb. tobo ordered to pay.
Colo Mottrom agt Rich Holden	Holden acks. Judgmt. 2204 lb tobo. Signed Richard Holden his marke.
Mr Wm Presly agt Rich Holden	Holden acks. Judgmt. 600 lb. tobo.

"Walter Weekes was sworne Constable for Chickacone"

Tho Hawkins agt Tho Kingwell	Referred to next Court in absence of Kingwell.
Peter Knight agt Edmond Perry his estate	Perry owing Knight 274 lb tobo. the Court orders payment from his estate.
Tho Wilsford agt Wm - - and John Davies	Referred to next Court.

37

Order Book #2.   21st November 1653.   page 19.

Henry Rocke cert for Land	"According to sufficient proofs made to this Court there is due to Henry Rocke - - acres of Land for the transportation of himself John Squibb and John - -es into this colony" Entry mutilated.
Simon Richardson Admr of Jeremy Alleine	"The Court doth order that a Com of Admr shall be granted to Simon Richardson of the estate of Jeremy Alleine decd x x"

Order Book #2.   21st November 1653.   page 20.

Tho Hawkins agt Martin Coles	Referred to next Court in Coles absence.
Wm Bedlam agt John Squibb	Referred to next Court.
Colo Mottrom agt Tho Hopkins	Col. Mottrom having arrested Hopkins the Court orders that if Hopkins does not appear by the next Court and answer the suit then order shall pass agst. his bail.
Hugh Lee agt Wm Thomas	Referred to next Court in Thomas absence.

Wm Thomas
his cert for Land
	200 acres due for transportation of the following into this colony:
	    Himselfe and ffrancis his wife
	    John ffrissell
	    Ann Parry

John Radford agt Martin Cole	"Whereas John Radford hath arrested Martin Cole to this Court and the said Cole doth not appear The Court doth order that if the said Cole do not appear the next Court and answere the suite then ord'r shall pass against his Baile"
Edward Cole agt Rich Span	Referred to next Court.

Order Book #2. 21st November 1653. page 20. This page mutilated.

Wm Warder
agt
- - fflynt

"Whereas x x by confession of Richard fflynt x x he x x hath sold x x three Cowes one heifer and one cowe calfe wch x x did belong to the said Richard fflynts wyfe and - - as by a deede - made to Wm - -er one of the - - be halfe o- - Mrs Dorathy fflynt and x x x solde by him - - in the said Deede of ffoeffmt and pay charges of Court else execution "

Peter Knight
agt
Mr Turney

Richard Turney having arrested Knight and not appearing against him is ordered to pay him 50 lb. tobo., and to pay Court charges.

Peter Knight
agt
John ffaucett

Faucett having arrested Knight and not appearing against him, is ordered to pay him 50 lb tobo., and to pay Court charges.

Mr Richard Cole
agt
Vincent Cox

"Whereas this cause is referred till the next Court and if the said Cox doe not then make appeare that the shipp in wch he came into this Country came to an anchor in Virginia on the 10th of Octo then he is to serve Mr Cole according to As- -emt and make good the time that he hath been out of Mr Coles his service "

Michael Tainler
agt
John Essex

John Essex owing Michael Tainler (Tainlew ?) 289 lb. tobo., is ordered to pay forthwith.

Thomas Knight
agt
Wm Thomas

Case referred to next Court.

John Walton
agt
Joseph Maning

Maning having arrested Walton to this Court and not having declared against him is ordered to pay him 50 lb. tobo. and to pay the Court charges.

Tho B--
agt
- -

This entry badly mutilated-too bad it was'ent torn away altogether.   " - - doth order - - Sherr of this - - agmt of - - for charges and - - expended in the b-ing over to - -mack Wm Vincent and Ann Moy (Mey, May ?) as felons out of the said Vinsents estate He the said Sherr paying himselfe his owne fees in the first place".

Note: It is none of our business at this late date as to how Willie and Annie disported themselves or who they ran away from, but we must not forget that this was the day of the Puritan . B.F.

Northumberland Co., Va. Court Order Book #2. 21st Nov. 1653. page 21.

Mrs Mary Calvert Confaced
"Whereas Mrs Mary Calvert hath confessed in Court That she hath Called the States and Keep's of the Liberty of England Rogues Traytors and Rebells in Mr Nicholas Morris his house Shee saith that at the time of speaking such words she was in great danger of her life being taken away by her husband and she spoke these words to no other end but onely to have some Magistrate or officer to secure her from her husband .The Court doth therefore Order that the said Mrs Calvert shall presently receav thirty stripes upon her bare shoulders fer this her offence Yet not withstanding upon Mr Calverts peticon in behalfe of his wife The Court doth Ord'r that the said Mr Calvert shall pay upon all demands to the account of the County one thousand pounds of Tobo and Caske for the Comuteing of the Corporall punishment to be inflicted upon this said wife with charges of Court else execution "

Note: Now Mrs. Calvert must have been well aware of what had taken place in Maryland. Colonel Claiborne had recently been a guest at the home of Colonel Mottrom. How was it possible that she could think otherwise than as she expressed herself? Whether those brutes expected to actually carry through this sentence or not we will never know, but it is plain that they frightened this gentlewoman into telling an untruth in Court. This Court scene must indeed have been elevating. The Puritans in all their Christian glory. Let us see exactly who these socalled men were. They were : Colonel John Mottrom, Mr John Trussell, Mr. William Presly, Mr. Nicholas Morris (Commissioners).   B. F.

Tho Hawkins his - - to James Macgregg'r
"The 22th Novem 1653 Tho Hawkins brought into the Court 13 pr of shoes and tendered them for the account of James Macgreggor according to an Ord'r of the last Court and was ready to pay forbearance and charges of Court"

Robt Lambdon agt Lt Coll ffletchers estate
"Att a Quarterly Court held at James Citty the 10th of October 1653 Richard Bennett Esq Governor and Colo Claybourne - - Colo Ludlow Lt Colo ffreman - - is ordered that Robert Lambdon to satisfy - - the estate of Lt Col ffletcher the sume of 9134 pounds of Tobaco and two barrells of Corne in his - - - place et Execuson   Ta/D Ro Huberd Cl Cor 22 Novem 1653 This Ord'r was Recorded "

The above entry mutilated.

Order Book #2.   22nd November 1653 (last date shown on record) page 21.

" Northumberland
Levies Ano 1653

To the publiq Levie at 15 lb per poll for 236 persons comes to	13.440
ffor carrying a Prison'r to Lancaster County	0.180
To Mr Budd for prevision for Mr ffletcher when he was Burgess	0.360
Mold for butter	0.120
for 11 Cheeses and a pale	0.360
for a man to row him to James Towne	0.600
for Wm Bedlams service	0.600
To Mr Brodhurst for Mr ffletchers uss	0.200
To the hire of a boate for the Burges and killing of a wolfe	0.600
To Mr Cetanceans and man for 4 dayes waiting on and charges	0.080
To Phillip Carpenter for a Canooe that was lost in the Counties service	0.030
To the Sherriffe for warning the freemen to choose Burgesses upon urgent occasion at 4 lb per poll	0.620
To Mr Smith for killing a Wolfe	0.100
To severall men that were prest to take Wm Vincent	0.150
To the Sherr for operating the Warrent	0.060
To John Haney for a Wolfe	0.100
To Arreares in 1652	0.874
for 3 persons that were gon and not paid their Levies at 85 lb per poll	0.255
for John - -(part of page missing) - at 3 lb per poll	0.708
for Max Mag- -ell	0.708
To Pillory for - - (part of page gone)	0.600

	18.705

Mr Smith was Collector for this Levie   "

Order Book #2. 26th February 1653/4. page 22.

"At a Court held for the County of Northumberland the 26th of
ffebruary 1653 "
Present   Colonel John Mottrom
               Mr John Trussell
               Mr Wm Presly
               Mr Nicho Morris
               Mr Wm Nash   Com'rs

Robt Sharpe   Thomas owing Sharpe 157 lb. tobo. and "three parts
agt   of a barrell of Corne" is ordered to pay within
Wm Thomas   ten days.

Mr Wm Presly   Order for payment to Presly of 584 lb. Tobo.
agt
Mr Edw Moores estate

Mr Richard Cole   "Whereas it doth appear unto the Court by the Deposi-
agt   tion of Wm Beesly and John Draper that Vincent Cox
Vincent Cox   came into this Country the 10th day of Octo last
                   was fower yeares and that the said Cox was solde or
assigned by John Pettitt to Mr Richard Cole for the serveing him the
said Mr Cole the remainder of fower yeares x x The Court doth order that
the said Cox shall be free x x" . Cole to pay charges.

Mr Nash   "According to sufficient proofs x x there is due
his cert for Land to Mr Wm Nash 700 acres of Land for the transporta-
                   tion of these persons following into this Colony"
                        Himselfe twice   John Merell
                        Ann his wife   Mex Cobra   (Mox ?)
                        John Godfrey   John Carter
                        Robt Stafford   Edw Sudbery
                        James Merrey   Mary Meares
                        Theodor Baker   Mary Blunstone
                        Thomas Pearce

Colo Mottrom   Case referred to next Court.
agt
John Ingram

Ann Moore   "According to sufficient proofs made to this
her cert for Land Court there is due to Ann Moore 100 acres of Land
                   for the transportation of herselfe and Ann her
                   daughter into this Colony "

James Claughton to   Claughton to have 150 lb. tobo. "x x for his going
have 150 lb of Tobo to the Indians out of the County Levies in Mr
                     Smiths hands ".

Order Book #2. 26th Feb. 1653/4   page 22.

Robert Lambdon agt Henry Wicher	Entry stained. Wicher owing Lambdon 428 lb tobo is ordered to pay within ten days.
Mr Hallowes agt Peter Knight	Case referred to next Court.

Rich Walker
agt
Phillip Carpenter
and Edw Henley
	Carpenter and Henley ack. Judgement 2100 lb. tobo, to be paid 10th Oct. next.
	    signed Phillip Carpenter
	            Edw Henley his marke

Rich Walker agt Edward Henley	Henley acks. Judgement 460 lb. tobo. to Walker to be paid Oct. 10th. signed Edward Henley his marke.
Mr Hallowes agt Tho Sheapard	John Powell attorney for Tho Sheapard acks Judgmt. 200 lb. tobo. to Mr Hallowes and 100 lb. by assignment from Mr. Speke. signed John Powell his mark.
John Radford agt Humfrey ffulford	Fulford acks. Judgmt. 600 lb tobo. to John Radford, to be paid 10th Nov. signed "the marke of Hum ffulford".
John Danby agt Mr Simpson	Thomas Wilsford, attorney of Mr. Paul Simpson, acks Judgement 556 lb. tobo. to John Danby.
Richard Budd agt Mr Calvert	"Whereas Mr Sampson Calvert Clerke doth owe unto Richard Budd" 1140 lb. tobo., David Spiller and Wm Spicer who are bound with Mr Calvert are ordered to pay within ten days.
John Davies agt Tho Wilsford	Davies having arrested Wilsford "to this Court in an ac'con of Diffamacon and canot prove the same" the Court orders the case dismissed.

Order Book #2. 26th Feb. 1653/4. page 23.

John Davies agt Tho Wilsford	Davies charges Wilsford with having attempted to collect 1260 lb. tobo. from him. Case dismissed and Davies ordered to pay charges.

43

Order Book #2.   Feb. 26th 1653/4   page 23.

John Davies
agt
Tho Wilsford

Case referred to next Court.

Richard White
agt
John Bradshaw

Bradshaw owing White 240 lb. tobo. ordered to pay.

John Bradshaw
agt
John Davies

The Court orders Davies to pay Bradshaw 40 lb tobo, for having him appear as witness agt. Wilsford.

Alex Magdoull
agt
Davies
Jon Bradshaw (sic)

"The Court orders that John Davies shall forthwith pay unto Alexander Magdoell 40 lb of tobo for his charge x x as a witnes x x agt Tho Wilsford x x "

Jno Henley
agt
John Davies

Davies to pay Henley 40 lb. tobo. as a witness.

Wm Reynolds
agt
John Davies

Davies to pay Reynolds 40 lb. tobo. as a witness.

Mr Morris
agt
Gervase Dodson

Case referred to next Court.

Jon Hull
agt
Jno Radford

"Whereas John Hull hath arrested John Radford to this Court and hath not declared against him" Hull is nonsuited and ordered to pay Radford 50 lb. tobo.

Jon Radford
agt
John Hull

Case referred to next Court.

John Bradshaw
agt
John Davies

Davies owing Bradshaw 240 lb tobo is ordered to pay forthwith.

Mr Nash
agt
Tho Pearce

Order that "Thomas Pearce shall serve his Master Mr Wm Nash for one yeare more to come since the 28 of January last and then be free he coming in without Indenture wch is according to Act of Assembly"

Order Book #2.   26th February 1653/4.   page 23.

John Kent
agt
Nathaniel Hickman

Hickman owing Kent 3 bbl. corn is ordered to pay forthwith.

Thomas Knight
agt
Wm Thomas

Thomas owing Knight 250 lb. yobo. is ordered to pay within ten days.

Edward Roberts
agt
Richard Holden

"Whereas x x by oaths of John Earle John Walker and Ann Ball that Thomas Dankington doth belong to and is the servant of Eadward Roberts x x the Court doth ord'r that x x Richard Holden shall deliver up the said Dankington forthwith x x "

John Walker
agt
Edward Roberts

Roberts ordered to pay Walker for appearing as a witness.

Ann Ball
agt
Edward Roberts

Roberts ordered to pay 40 lb. tobo. to Ann Ball as a witness.

Order Book #2.   26th Feb 1653/4.   page 24.

Jno Earle
agt
Edward Roberts

Roberts ordered to pay Earle as a witness.

Seth Foster
agt
Wm Hardich

Hardich owing Foster 2hhds of Tobo. the Court orders "that forasmuch as the said Hardich liveth in another County that an attachment shall be granted him (Foster) for the attachment of 2 hhds of Tobo in Wm Reynolds his hands of the estate of the said Hardiches "

Seth ffoster
agt
Corbet Podle

To next Court in Podle's absence.

Thos Sheapard
agt
Tho Hawkins

It appears "by oath of James Claughton that Thomas Sheapard did deliver backe to Thomas Hawkins one paire of bootes". The Court orders "Hawkins shall abate soe much out of his debt ".

Order Book #2. 26th February 1653/4. page 24.

Wm Bedlam agt John Squibb	" x x if John Squibb doe not appear the next Court then ord'r shall pass agt him for a hhd of Tobo for things that he took out of the said Bedlams house "
Peircy Hamond agt Tho Wilsford	Case referred to next Court.
Colo Mottrom agt David Spiller	"Whereas x x John Dennis Senr doth owe unto Mr Tho Speke 330 lb. tobo. x x the Court doth order that David Spiller who married with the widdow and Adm x x of the said Dennis shall within ten days make payment x x ".
Mr Simpson agt Mr Hayward	"Whereas Mr Thos Lun atturney of Mr Nicholas Hayward did arrest Mr Paul Simpson to this Court and doth not declare against him", the case is dismissed and Lun ordered to pay Simpson 50 lb.tobo.
David Spiller agt Rich fflynt	Case referred to next Court in Flint's absence.
Rich Budd David Spiller Tho Gaskins and Jo Gresham agt Mr Calvert	"Whereas Mr Sampson Calvert hath arrested Richd Budd David Spiller Tho Gaskins and Jo Gresham to this Court and doth not declare against them" the Court declares Calvert nonsuited and to pay 50 lb. tobo to each.

Mr Nicholas Morris   "We whose names are underwritten being impannelled
agt   to trye a difference depending between Mr Nicholas
Isobel Salsbury   Morris pltiff and Isobel the wife of Thomas Salis-
                      bury Defendt Doe Award that both Pltiffe and De-
fendt shall pay their owne charges and that the suite now Depending shal
be finally p'er'wded.

Hugh Lee	Tho Brewer	Geo Nott
Wm Thomas	Antho Linton	Rich Gibble
Peter Presly	Wm Reynolds	Rob Smith
Richard Loyd	Robt Lambdin	Geo Courtnell

26 ffeb 1653 This Verdict was Recorded   "   (1653/4)

Order Book #2.   26th February 1653/4.   page 24.

Colonel Mottrom "Whereas we whose names are underwritten being im-
agt   pannelled to trye a difference x x between Colo John
Tho Hopkins   Mottrom pltiff and Tho Hopkins Defendt concerning
                 a - - Doe awarde that the said Hopkins shall deliver
the said Cow mentioned in the bill of sale with all her increase that
are living unto the said Colo Mottrom x x"
" Wm Thomas   John Earle   Hen Moseley
   Mich Brooke   Walter Weekes   David Spiller
   James Claughton   Robt Sharpe   John Howard
   Robt Smith   Geo Courtnell   John Kent
26 ffeb 1653 This Verdict was Recorded "   (1653/4)

Capt Tho Hackett A case in which a bill of Hackett's for 1000 lb of
agt   tobo is declared invalid.
Hugh Lee   The Jury:
   Wm Thomas   Richard Budd   James Claughton
   Tho Gaskins   Tho Brewer   Rich Gible
   John Earle   John Powell   John Aires
   John Walton   James Willis   Rich Holden
"26 ffeb 1653 this Verdict was Recorded"   (1653/4)

Mr Nicho Morris   "we whose names are underwritten being impannelled
agt   to trye - - suite between Mr Nicholas Morris and
Henry Wicher   Henry - - - - that - Morris shall pay unto the said
                  Wic- - - of Tobo and Caske - - and said Wichor prov-
ing his peticon against the   said Morris sufficiently prov- - - nothing
against the said Wicher   And wee doe further Awarde a finale period to
this case or suite now in difference
   Wm Thomas   John Aires   Rich Holden
   Rich Budd   Tho Brewer   Tho Gaskins
   James Claughton   John Walton   John Earle
   John Powell   Rich Gibble   James Willis
26th ffeb 1653 This Verdict was Recorded   "   (1653/4)

Arthur Branch   "The Deposition of Arthur Branch aged 28 yeares
his Depo   taken the 17th of January 1652 (sic) Arthur Branch
                 being at Mr Morrises with other company was called
out to help part the said - -ice and Henry Wicher Martin Cole and
Abraham Byram all a fighting the sa- Morris giving the said Branch a
rope saying I will bind - - and - - and the said Branch laying downe
the rope - - the said Morris wth out - -eld and the said Wicher - - - -
Morris said he would - - and struck up - - of the said Wicher fell - -
and the said Mor- - -tine Cole called for the rope and the said Branch
told them it was gon The said Branch tooke holde of the said Wichor and
ledd him downe towards the water side and gott him into the - - - to
have him home and as - - said Branch and Wicher were goeing there came
the said Cole and others and took the said Wicher from the said Branch
and brought him the said Wicher to the said Morrises - - and kept him
there all night and further saith not The Marke of Arthur Branch Jurat
Coram me Geo ffletcher   "
The foregoing record mutilated, parts of page missing. The date is doubtless January 1653/4 instead of the 1652 shown in the original.

Order Book #2. 26th February 1653/4.   page 25. This page mutilated, stained and part missing.

Isabel Salsbury   "Isabel Salsbury aged 30 years or thereabouts taken
her Depo   the 17th of January 1652 (sic) saith that she was
                   at Mr Morrises and there was divers people in the
house of the said Morris a drincking and the said Morris and Henty
Wicher were in another room and the said Morris swore and called the
said Wicher dog - - I will make - - know where you are and before whom
you speak and I went out with severall others to see what - - matter
was and shee the said Salsbury found the said Wicher upon the ground
and the said Morris upon him the - Morris ran out and said he would
fetch a rope and pull the said Wicher neck and heels and Mrs Morris
parted her husband and prayed him to be quiett for he the said Morris
was a Lemi- - the said Wicher - - from amongst - - - - said thou
Rogue - - - (page mutilated and partly missing here) - - - from the
Indians but no - - - all and with that run upon the - - and threw him
the said Wicher downe and fell upon him the said Wicher and Martin Cole
tooke hold of the said Wicher and - -uled him the said Wicher And
Arthur Branch took hold of the said Wicher to carry him away downe to
the Canoe to have him home and the said Cole run after the said Wicher
to have him back to the said Morrises house for he would have him necke
and heels he the - - having ropped (or ressled) the J- - Arthur Branch
and Thomas Scoggin tooke the said Wycher from the said Cole to have him
home and Martin Cole and Abraham Byram - - hands upon the said Wicher
and tooke him the said Wicher from the said Branch and Scoggin and they
would have him prisoner at the said Morryes house Mrs Morris came
downe to the Waters side and said he was no Outlaw haveing a house to
goe to and the said Cole swore by God he should goe with them to be a
prisoner except he the said Wicher - - - in good - - and Samuel Smith
High Sherriff said he would - his bayle for 5000 lb of Tobo and - -nd
Cole swore he would not have less than 10- Tobo and the said Smith
with others came and - - - Wichers saying the said Morris was my - - -
and said he would not stay in the house except the - - Wichers was
broaght prisoner to his house and - - saith not The - - of Isabel
Salsbury
26 ffeb 1653 This Depo was Recorded "   (1653/4)

Note: The date in this deposition is shown as 1652 in the original. This date was nevertheless doubtless 1653/4, as in the deposition of Arthur Branch. B.F.

Thomas Reade   "Thomas Reade aged 29 yeares sworn and examined - -
his Depo   Being at the house of Thomas Salisbaries upon a - -
                  about Tobo Henry Wichers - - Mr Morris at was - - -
of cheating tricks of a - - Morris after him - - then call me cheating
- - - his answere was- - can you make better of it than a cheate and
further saith not Tho Reade ffeb 14 1653 Wm Nash 16 ffeb 1653 This
Depo was recorded "

Note: While the record is badly damaged still perhaps not as much so as Henry Wicher was at the time. Quite a fancy party for Puritans at Judge Morris' house.   B.F.

47

Order Book #2. 26th February 1653/4. page 25.

Anthony Linton agt Wm Thomas	Thomas owing Linton 300 lb tobo ordered to pay forthwith. Signed Jno Trussell, Wm Presly.

"Mr Wm Presly was sworne high Sherriffe of this county of Northumberland - - - John Trussell"

Order Book #2. 20th July 1654. page 26.

"At a Court held for the County of Northumberland the 20th of July 1654
Present
    Colo John Mottrom
    Mr John Trussell
    Mr Sam Smith
    Mr Nicho Morris
    Mr Wm Nash   Com'rs   "

Tho Brewer agt John Prosser	Brewer to have an attachment agt the estate of Prosser "he being departed the County" for "the payment of one table and forms x x by Bill x x"
John Radford agt Martin Cole	"Whereas x x Martin Cole should give and deliver unto Thomas Darrow or his assigns 160 acres of Land by Covenant und'r his hand" the Court orders Cole to deliver the land forthwith to John Radford assignee.
John Powell agt Joseph Maning	This entry mutilated. "Whereas it doth appear x x by x Deposition of Mr John Hallowes and John Walton that Joseph Maning was imployed by Mr - - - and Mr Chichester and that the said Maning - - Bill - - -

name in Selliacks name or in Mr Chichesters name and whereas it doth appear by the oathes of Robert Lowe and Thomas Phillips that the said Maning did hire a sloope of John Powell and did not return the same againe but by his neglect was made unservicable and little worth The Court doth now ord'r that in respect the Sloop was hired for the getting in of Mr Chichesters Mr Sellincks and his owne Tobo and meate That Mr Charles Ashton shall by the 20th of Novem next make paymt of 1000 lb of Tobo and caske with charges of Court unto John Powell for his said sloope x x "

Vincent Cox agt Mr Richard Cole	The Court orders Cole to pay to Vincent Cox, his late servant, one cloth suit, one pair of shoes and stockings, one shirt, one hat or cap and three barrels of Indian corn, being due unto him, by Oct 20th.

Order Book #2.   20th July 1654.   page 26.

Robt Sharpe agt Jo Davies	Davies ordered to pay Sharpe 30 lb. tobo for being witness.

ffran Simons agt John Davies	Davies ordered to pay Simons 30 lb. tobo. for being witness agt. Tho. Wilsford.

Tho Orlys Answer to Mr Preslys Poll in Chancery

"The Answere of Tho Orly to the Bill of Complaint of Mr Wm Presly being sworne and examined saith That the gun of Mr Edward Moores was carried away by Hen Barnes from this -dents house   This - - hath 500 of six penny nailes of the estate of Mr Moores in his hands   The Land whoever this - - - received of Mrs Moore an old peece of a cotton petticote cutt and made up into a wastcote a canvas sheete to make a pr of drawers and a shirt off   He this - - hath of the said Mr Moores a Cert for 900 Acres of Land And further canet Answere   Thomas Orley"

Note: Now we have more of Mr. Presly, Mr. Orley, the gunn and the canvas   drawers. The wastcote seems to have been overlooked. B.F.

Mr Wm Presly agt Tho Orley

"The Court doth Ord'r That Tho Orley shall by the 20 of Novem next pay 100 lb tobo for the shirt and the - - he had of Mrs Moore and 500 - - - unto Mr Wm Presly and that the - - - shall take into his custody and possession Cert for 900 acres of Land due to Mr Edward Moore - - - delivered up in Court and it was ordered that if ever the Gun came to the said Orleys hands that then he shall deliver it to the said Mr Presly in part of satisfaction for a greater sume of Tobo x x In case the said Mr Presly shall meete with Hen Barnes who carried away the gun It is ordered that he shall take possession him-selfe of the said gunn "

Tho Gerrard his certif for Land

According to sufficient proofs, etc., 100 acres due Garrard for transportation to this colony of:
    Mary Wesson
    Christopher - - .

James Maggregor Attur of - - agt Colo Mottrom

Case   referred to next Court.

Matthew Rhodon his Cert for Land

According to proofs, etc., Rhodon to have 300 acres for transportation of following to this colony:
    Hum - - -
    Geo Curmickelle
    Max Makewater   (Note: What a name !
    Daniel Glover   would'ent have believed
    Sarah Read   it unless I'd seen it
    Wm Wiles   myself. B.F.)

Order Book #2. 20th July 1654. page 27.

John Haney Attur   Referred to next Court.
of Adam Westgate
agt
Wm Thomas

Wm Thomas   Referred to next Court.
agt
Mr Morris   (Note: While this type
                                                         of entry is a great bore
                                                         a nuisance and takes up
Thomas Shaw   Referred to next Court.   time and space that we
agt   would like to devote to
Anthony Linton   other things, still this
                                                         detail must be included
Seth Foster   Referred to next Court.   to make the record com-
agt   plete.   B.F.)
Mr Sam Smith

Wm Botts   "Whereas Wm Botts did enter into bond with Mary
agt   Purnell for the payment of a debt of 1500 lb. of
Michael Brooke   tobo. and cask unto Thomas Stephens and the debt is
                         not satisfied soe that the said Botts is liable to
the suite of the said Stephens and Michael Brooke who married with the
said Purnell is departed this colony   The Court doth order that the
said Botts shall have an attachment agt the estate of the said Michael
Brooke wth the Lands of John Haney for his security for - - him harmles
from the said debt with charges of Court "

Hugh Lee   Referred to next Court.
agt
John Hulet

Wm Thomas Attur   Edward Hull owing John Michael attorney of Jacob
of John Michael   Simonson 580 lb. tobo. Hull not appearing and a
Admr of Jacob   former order granted agt. Thos Hawkins for the said
Simonson   Hull's bail, the Court orders Hawkins to pay Thomas
agt   by Nov. 20th.
Thos Hawkins

John Haney   Pritchett owing 500 lb. tobo to Haney is ordered to
agt   pay by Oct. 20th.
Tho Pritchett

Tho Broughton   Podle having arrested Broughton to this Court and
agt   not declaring against him is ordered to pay Brough-
Corbet Podle   ton 50 lb. tobo and costs.

Order Book #2.   20th July 1654, page 27.

Mr Morris agt Isobell Salisbury	"The Court doth order that all differences between Mr Morris and Isabell Salisbury and between Isobell Salisbury and Mr Morris shall be ended and both of them hereunto gives their consent x x x if the said Isabel Salisbury shall at any time hereafter abuss the said Mr Morris she shal be severely punished according to law "

Note: The Hon'ble Com'r seems to have resented Mrs. Salisbury's kindly remarks concerning Mrs. Morris' conduct at his entertainment this past January. And if Mrs. Salisbury had any doubt as to the law in the hands of the Puritans, all she had to do was to ask Mrs Calvert. We can but hope that she took the hint from the Court and shut up.   B.F.

Tho Gaskins agt David Spiller	"The Court doth order That Mr Dodson shall goe downe and see what the difference is betweene them and that he take with him John Gresham Richard Budd Tho Hopkins John Waddy and report the difference to the next Court "
Tho Yorke agt Geo Berry	Referred to next Court in Berry's absence.
Mr Morris agt Hen Wicher	"The Court of Chancery doth ord'r and Decree That the Hhd of Tobo Mr Morris was cost in the last Court at the said Wichers suite shal be remitted And that all differences betweene them shal be ended and that they pay each of them there owne charges "

Note: If the jury could not see Mr Morris' viewpoint then he knew very well who could. Mr. Com'r does not appear in the romantic Virginia tradition.   B.F.

David Spiller agt Rich fflynt	The petition of David Spiller. The Court having ordered paymt. of 334 lb. tobo. to Col. Jno.Mottrom from the estate of John Dennis, deceased, "your

petitioner humbly craves the - ord'r against Richard fflynt according to his Conn- - with costs of suite and your petitioner shall pray - - - Wee those names are underwritten being impannelled on a Jury between David Spiller pltiff and Rich fflynt Defent Doe Awarde that the Pltiff shall have his debt paid him from the said Defent the last day of Novem next with charges of Court - - the debt appears to be due - - jointly- - to the - - Spiller as Admr of John Dennis - - our hands the - of July 1654. "

John Haynie	Tho - -	Hen Rayner	
Tho - -	Rich - -	Tho Coggin	
John - -	Walter -	Wm Medcalf	
John - -	John Bayles	Tho - -	(entry mutilated)

Order Book #2. 20th July 1654. page 28.

John Radford
agt
John Hull

"Wee whose names are underwritten being impannelled to trye a difference between John Radford Chyrurgion Pltiffe and John Hull Defendt we do Awarde the Pltiffe his full accompt and the Defendt 235 pounds of Tobo of his accompt in full And wee doe further Awarde that the said Defendt shall pay to the said Pltiffe the surplusage of his accompt being the - of Twelve hundred twenty five pounds of Tobo with all charges expended in the said suite by the last day of Novemb next In witnes that this is our verdict wee have sett our hands the 20th of July 1654 "

  John Haynie Wm Botts Hen Rayner
  James Hawley Edward Roberts Matth Rhodon
  Wm Thomas Wm Wildey Walter Weeks
  Rich fflynt Wm Little Tho Shaw

Order Book #2. 22 August 1654. page 28.

A Caveat agt
the Ad'con - of
Tho Baldridge

"22 Aug 1654
Let no will be proved nor Ad'con granted nor anything also be done in the estate of Thomas Baldridge till John Tew who married with Grace Boman the then betrothed wife of the said Baldridge and principal creditor to the estate be first called"

Note: The above names may be John Tow and Grace Beman just as well. The very fine handwriting in the original, at times not so large as this type, makes it often impossible to differentiate between the small 'e' and the small 'o' of the 17th Century Court Hand. B.F.

Order Book #2. 20th November 1654. page 28.

"At a Court held for the County of Northumberland the 20th day of Novem 1654
Present Colo John Mottrom
  Mr Sam Smith
  Mr Nicho Morris
  Mr Wm Nash
  Mr Wm Reynolds Com'rs "

Hugh Lee
agt
Tho Hayles

Hales acks. Judgmt. 986 lb. tobo. to Hugh Lee. Signed Tho Hailes his mark.

Tho Reade
agt
John Prosser

"Whereas Thomas Reade had an Attachmt against the estate of John Prosser and by virtue thereof one Bull Collared black pyde - - " to be given into the possession of Reade.

Order Book #2. 20th November 1654. page 28.

Tho Wilsford his cert for Land
x x 100 acres of land due for transportation of the following into the colony:
Sarah Southorne
Judith Southorne

John Kent agt Geo Courtnell
Courtnell owing Kent 1150 lb. tobo. ordered to pay.

"David Spiller is appointed Constable for great Wicocomocoe and it is ordered that he take his oath before a Com'r there"

Ralph Horsley agt John Squibb
"x x a Jackett and a gun was attached by Ralph Horsley of John Squibbs x x shall be appraised and that the said Horsley shall take them into his owne possession for the payment of nine paire of french heeld and wooden heeled shoes " and 243 lb. tobo. due unto him by Bill from Squibb.

Note: Even today we would consider a gun and a jacket a safer bet in Northumberland Co. than French heeled shoes.   B.F.

Tho Brewer agt Simon Cox
Cox owing Brewer 1000 lb. tobo. and Cox being arrested and not appearing "The Court doth Ord'r that if Martine Cole who is his Baile doe not bring forth the body of the said Cox unto the next Court then order shall pass against him the said Cole x x "

Note: There is an unpleasant suggestion about these orders. Bring in the body, nevermind the soul.   B.F.

John Waddy to Keepe an Ordinary
"The Court orders that John Waddy shall have Liense to keepe an Ordinary towards the head of great Wicocomocoe till he gett further Ord'r from the Govern'r and Councell at James Citty "

ffran Simons Ad'mor of Wm Peirce
Order that Francis Simons have certificate of Admr. on estate of William Peirce, deceased.

Thos Wilsford agt Edw Henley
Henley owing Wilsford 313 lb. tobo. ordered to pay forthwith.

Wm Addams agt Henry Moseley
Moseley owing Adams 500 lb. tobo. ordered to pay Mr. Tho. Speke, assignee of Adams.

Order Book #2.   20th November 1654.   page 29.

Wm Light agt Colo Jo Mottrom	Mottrom acks. Judgmt. 600 lb. tobo. unto James Macgregger, attorney of Wm Light. 　　　　　Signed. John Mottrom.
Wm Hardich agt Geo Courtnell	Wm Addams owing Wm Hardich 670 lb. tobo., the Court orders Courtnell, who went bail for Addams, to pay by Nov. 20th.
Geo Courtnell agt Wm Addams	Order that Adams pay Courtnell 670 lb. tobo. for forfeited bail.
Ro Vaulx agt Rich fflynt	Flint acks. Judgmt. 1200 lb. tobo. to Robert Vaulx, "allways provided that Mr Broughton - - what he hath given under his hand and is recorded Ri fflynt "
Tho Sheapard agt Daniel ffoxcroft	Case referred to next Court.
Tho Hawkins his cert for Land	100 acres due for transportation of the following into this colony: 　　　Mary Bayly 　　　Wm Conger
Colo Mottrom agt John Raven	Raven acks. Judgmt. 1015 lb tobo to Col. Mottrom. 　　　　Signed John Raven his mark.
Colo Mottrom agt Rich fflynt	Flint acks. Judgmt 810 lb. tobo. to Col. Mottrom. 　　　　Signed Rich fflynt.
Hen Cartwright agt Tho Hailes	Case referred to next Court.
Rob Booth agt Anth Linton	Linton owing Booth 428 lb. tobo. is ordered to pay Tho Shaw, assignee of Booth.
Anth Linton agt Tho Shaw	Case referred to next Court.

Order Book #2. 20th November 1654. page 29.

Eliza Newman agt Capt Tho Burbage	There being 900 lb. tobo. belonging to the estate of Capt. Thomas Burbage, in the hands of Mr Sam Smith, and this being attached by Mrs. Elizabeth Newman toward payment for a cow and calf, and this being duly proved by the depositions of Wm Cornish and Wm Gookin, the Court orders payment to Mrs. Newman.
Henry Moseley agt Wm Addams	Referred to next Court.
Tho Wilkinson agt Mr Presly	John Earle owing Thomas Wilkinson 300 lb. tobo. and being arrested to this Court and not appearing, the Court orders that Presly bring the body of Earle to the next Court or pay to John Hull, assignee of Wilkinson.
Wm Medcalf agt Corbet Podle	Podle arresting Medcalfe and not appearing against him, is nonsuited and ordered to pay Medcalfe 50 lb tobo.
Seth ffoster agt Mr Smith	Corbet Podle owing Seth Foster 700 lb. tobo., being arrested and not appearing, in default of Mr. Smith not taking bail. the Court orders Smith to pay Foster.

page 30.

Mr Smith agt Corbet Podell	The Court having ordered Mr. Sam Smith to pay 700 lb. tobo. to Seth Foster, now orders Podell to pay Smith.

Order Book #2. 20th November 1654. page 30.

Colo Mottrom agt Jo Larrett	Tho Saffall owing Mottrom 300 lb. tobo. and he not appearing, the Court orders Larrett who gave bail, to pay.
Colo Mottrom agt Mr Starkey	Referred to next Court.
Colo Mottrom agt John Haney	"Whereas John Haney hath in his custody a gun of Colo John Mottroms which was taken from an Indian about two or three years ago and by Act of Assembly Indemnity is granted to all persons that have lent guns to Indians The Court doth order that for that reason the said John Haney shall forthwith deliver the said gun unto the said Colo Mottrom else execution"

Order Book #2.   20th November 1654.   page 30.

Alice Shaw agt Tho Haile	Alice Shaw having been called as a witness for Tho Haile agt. Anthony Linton, Haile is ordered to pay her 50 lb. tobo.
Mr Knight agt Wm Jones	Mr. Peter Knight to have attachment agt. estate of Wm Jones for 1500 lb. tobo. due to Mr. Edward Bland in the hands of Hugh Lee.
Colo Mottrom his cert for Land	250 acres of land due for transportation of the following into the colony: "2 Scotts and 3 Irish bought out of Mr Warrens shipp and Capt Swanleys shipp "
Mr Smith agt Hannah Span	Referred to next Court.
Mr Smith agt Rich Span	Referred to next Court.
Mr Knight agt Colo Mottrom	Referred to next Court.
Tho Hawkins agt Hugh Lee	Referred to next Court.
Mr Newman his Cert for Land	650 acres due to Mr Robert Newman "Assigned to him by John Branch and the cert was lost and no land ever taken up by virtue of the former cert as the said Mr Newman deposed for the transportation of these persons following into the colony Vizt: John Branch Wm Warwell Mary his wife Tho Parkes Mary his daughter Walter Prichard Edw Toogood Rich Grigson David Griffin Rob Swaile John Willis John Clew Wm Wade

The next entry in Order Book #2 is dated July 21st 1655.   See page 57.

Order Book #2. July 21st 1655. page 30.

July 21st 1655   "ffor the better setling and apointing of a Markett
Markett Places   place in our countie of Northumberland wee doe
Appointed   Order and apoint wth the Major Consent of the in-
                      habitants as ffoll
      Att great Wickacomycoe the m'yett place is apointed and the bounds
thereof fro the creeke - - known by the name of Knights Creeke and soe
to extend to deep Creek in Mr Morrises Land -
   at Little Wickacomycoe fro the Bridge Creeke to Allens Creek
     Att Chickacoan fro the mouth of Chicacoan Riv'r to the plantacon
of Coll John Mottrom Decd (sic) from honist point to the Oyster shel
point and manie pt of the neck for farr as the house of Mr Mathew
Rhoden and on the other side of Chickacoan River and upon the south-
erlie side of Cherry Point neck to the Gleab Land at Yawmicoe fro
Youcomicoe to the house of Richd Holden
                    Nich Morris   Richd Budd
                    James Hawley   Matth Rhoden "

Note: According to this Colonel John Mottrom is now dead. B.F.

Order Book #2. 20th August 1655. page 31.

"Att a Court held for the County of Northumberland the 20th day of
August 1655
Present   Maj'er Samuel Smyth   Capt Rich'd Budd
            Mr Will'm Nash   Mr Hugh Lee
            Mr James Hawley   Capt John Rogers
                 Mr Matth Rhoden   Com'rs "

"This daye Mr Hugh Lee was sworne a Comissioner"

Francis Symonds   Francis Symonds, Admr. of Est. of Wm Priece, deceas-
his Quietus est   ed, having submitted a/c to the Court, and having
upon Wm Pricce   paid out more than the estate by 1530 lb. tobo.,
his estate   to have Quietus est.

Mr Hugh Lee   Lee to have certificate of Admr. on estate of
Ad'mr Robt Sharpe   Robert Sharpe, deceased.

Rich Holden   200 acres due for transportation of following into
his cert for   this colony.
Land   John Gibbins
                      Elizabeth Clifton
                      an Irish woman called Joane
                      Jane Brorlett (?)

Tho Saffall   Referred to next Court.
agt   John Prosser

Order Book #2. 20th August 1655. page 31.

John Kent agt Mr Hugh Lee	Lee owing Kent for a servant is ordered to pay 1580 lb tobo by Nov. 10th.
Avis Hickman Admr of Nath Hickman	Avis Hickman to have cert. of Admr. of estate of Nathaniel Hickman, her late husband, deceased.
Mr Lee agt Wm Allerson	Hugh Lee to have attachment agt the estate of Wm Allerson for 765 lb. tobo.
Mr Lee agt Avis Hickman Admr Nath Hickman	Nathaniel Hickman owing Lee 434 lb. tobo., Avis Hickman, Admr., ordered to pay by Nov. 10th.
Deb Allerson to dispose of a parcel of Hoggs	The Court orders that Deborah Allerson shall have the privilege of disposing of a parcel of hogs belonging to her husband, that are now on the plantation of Thos Walter.
Francis Symons agt Seth Foster	Referred to next Court.
Mr Wilsford agt Avis Hickman Admr of Nath Hickman	Hickman owing Wilsford "for Levies and fees" 121 lb. tobo., Avis Hickman, Admr. ordered to pay by Nov. 10th.
- - - Ad'tor Wm Ginsey agt Abraham Moone	Abraham Moone owing Wm Ginsey, deceased, by specialty and also by ack. of Seth Foster, attorney of Moone 3 cows etc.-the Court orders Moone to pay and deliver to Mr. Nicholas J- - , Admr. of Wm. Ginsey.
Avis Hickman 10 lb Tobo the ann of every freeman for transport over the Creek	"Whereas Avis Hickman widow is very much troubled in setting people over the creek by her house The Court doth order that of every Freeman she transports over the said creek she shall receive tenn pounds of Tobo yearly "
Seth Foster agt Avis Hickman Ad'r of Nathaniel Hickman	Avis Hickman, Administratrix of est. of Nathaniel Hickman, acks. Judgmt. for paymt. of 300 lb. Tobo. on 10th Nov. 1655 to Seth Foster.

Order Book #2.   20th August 1655.   page 31.

Martin Cole "Whereas Sarah Kingwell widdow being left in a very
agt   sad condition altogether destitute of any help and
Tho Kingwell nowe at the house of Martin Cole the Court doth
             order that for soe long time as she remains at the
sd Coles house hee the sd Cole shall have reasonable satisfaction out
of the estate of Thos Kingwell deceased according to order of recovery
els execution"

Hen Mayes   "Wee whose names are underwritten being impannelled
agt   on a Jury in a difference between Henry Mayes pltiff
Capt Richd Budd and Capt Richd Budd defent Wee doe Awarde that the
                Defent shall acknowledge that he hath done the
pltife wrong or else paye unto the plantiffe six hundred pounds of tobo
and caske fine and the charges - to the Court

    John Haynie   Thomas Lumpkin   John Gublin
    Wm Presly   Richd Holden   Thomas Prichett
    John Motteram   Richard Gibb   Martin Cole
    John Gresham   John Radford   Richd Raymond

John Hopper   "John Hopper aged 25 yeares or thereabouts sworne
his Depo   and examined sayeth that Mr Budd being at David
              Spillers house meeteing Henry Mayes there told
Henry Mayes hee heard hee had taken an oath agt him that the simth was
to have the shopp for two or three yeares and that he was to have
beere stand by him in the shopp same times Henry Mayes said he had
taken an oath to that purpose Mr Budd replyed it was a false oath and
hee would prove it and further saith not John Hopper his marke June
the 18th 1655 Will Nash "

David Spiller "David Spiller aged 36 yeares or thereabouts sworne
his Depo   and examined sayeth the same that John Hopper doth
               and further sayeth not David Spiller his marke
               June the 18th 1655 Will Nash

Henry Mayes   Capt Richd Budd acknowledges in Court in having
agt   done Henry Mayes wrong in saying he had taken a
Capt Rich Budd false oath.

Capt Rich Budd The Court orders in settlement of a/c betw. Budd
agt   and Mayes that Mayes pay Court charges in the suit.
Henry Mayes

Richard Clare   "and was sworn in Court"
Constable for
Chickacoan

Order Book #2. 20th August 1655. page 32.

Thos Brewer agt Martin Cole	"Whereas it was ordered at a Court held the 20th of Novemb 1654 that if Martin Cole did not bring forth the body of Symon Cox unto the next Court

after the said Cole being his baile that the order shoul pass agt the said Cole for 1000 lb. tobo. and caske being due from said Cox by Bill unto Thos Brewer ". Cox not appearing Cole is ordered to pay by 10th November.

Geo Nutt Ad8er of John Kaye	George Nott to have certificate of Admr on estate of John Kaye, deceased.
Mr Wilsford agt Geo Nott Admr of John Kaye	Kaye owing Wilsford 68 lb. tobo. his Adm'r ordered to pay.
Wm Presly agt Geo Nott Ad'mr of John Kaye	Kaye owing Presly 75 lb. tobo., his Adm'r ordered to pay.
Edward Coles agt John Prosser	"Whereas it doth appear unto the Court that John Prosser doth owe unto Edward Coles one Table five foote and fower inches in length two foote and halfe

over with a forme suteable to the sd Table and likewise to sett up and make benches round the Table and the said Prosser being arrested and not appearing The Court doth therefore order that if John Gamblin who is his Baile doe not bring forth the body of the said Prosser unto the next that then order shall pass agt him the said Gamblin for the preformeance of the premisses with charges of Court "

Seth Foster Att of Tho Haukins agt Edwd Hudson	Referred to next Court.
John Motteram his cert for Land	50 acres due for transportation of himself into the colony.
Ralph Horsley Att of Thomas Lund Att of Mr Nich Hayward agt Mr Trussell	Referred to next Court.
Mr Knight agt Laurence Damorell	The Court orders that Laurence Damorell shall by the next Court deliver up to Mr Peter Knight his bond concerning the acknowledgement of a Patent of Land which x x Mr Knight hath acknowledged in Court.

Order Book #2. August 20th 1655. page 32.

John Gresham agt John Hopper	Hopper owing Gresham 896 lb. tobo. ordered to pay.
Geo Courtnell agt Wm Little	Case referred to next Court.
John Gresham his Quietus est upon John Abbots estate	John Gresham, Admr of the estate of John Abbot, deceased, having submitted a/c, etc., given Quietus est.
Mr Goche agt Wm Thomas Attur of John Gatehouse	Thomas ordered to pay 300 lb. tobo. to Jeffery Goche.
John Hopper agt Wm Thomas	"Whereas it doth appear unto me that Wm Thomas of Yeocomoco doth owe unto John Hopper" 125 lb. tobo. he is ordered to pay. Signed Hugh. Lee.
Mr Wilsford his Quietus est for Collecting of the Levies	"Whereas Mr Thomas Wilsford hath given up his accompt for the Levies in the year 1652 wherein he was Collector", the Court orders him his Quietus est.
Rich Gibbe his cert for Land	50 acres due for transportation of Wm Jones into this colony.
Mr Knight agt Jno Hopper	"Whereas Peter Knight was summoned to this Court to declare himself upon oath at which time John Hopper interrupted the sd Mr Knight and taxed him with swearing falsely." The Court orders Hopper to pay Knight 300 lb. tobo. by Nov. 10th
James Claughton agt Thomas Phillpott att of Hen Cartwright	"Whereas James Claughton informed the Court that he was arrested at the suite of Thomas Philpott Atturney of Henry Cartwright and the said Phillpot does not declare against him", The Court declares Phillpot nonsuited, etc.
Ri fflynt agt Freeman Conaway	"This cause is referred till the next Court by the request of James Aston Attorney of Mr George Cololough security for Conaways appearance at this court"
Mr Radford exempted from the Levies	"The Court doth order that de futuro Mr John Radford shall be exempted from paying the County and Country Levies hee being above the age of sixty yeares " (Note: Therefore born circa 1595. B.F.)

Order Book #2. 20th August 1655, page 32.

Anthony Linton "We whose names are underwritten being impannelled
agt   to try a difference depending between Anthony
Tho Shawe   Linton p'lt'iff and Thomas Shawe defendt do award
                that Anthony Linton shall pay the Juries charges
and Thomas Shawe all other Court Charges

    Wm Thomas   James Claughton   George Courtnell
    John Radford   Symon Richdson   Richd Rice   (sic)
    Walter Weekes   Richd Clarke   Richd Rice   (sic)
    John Walker   Robert Such   David Spiller   "

Tho Hawkins   "We whose names are underwritten " etc., award that
agt   the defent. pay the pltf. 600 lb. tobo.
John Barnes
    Wm Thomas   James Claughton   Geo Courtnell
    Wm Presly   John Radford   David Spiller
    Rich Clarke   Richd Rice   Robert Such
    John Walker   Tho Walter   Symon Richardson

Order Book #2. 20th August 1655. page 33.

John Hayles   "Wee whose names are underwritten being impannelled
agt   to try a difference between Hanah Lee Atturney for
Mr Trussell   John Hayles an Orphant and Mr John Trussell doe
               award that the said Trussell shall pay one cow
calfe valued the last spring unto the said Hayles or any one whom hee
shall appoint betweene this and Christmas next Allsoe charges of Court"

    Wm Thomas   John Motteram   Henry Mayes
    John Haynie   Tho Prichett   Richard Clare
    John Gresham   George Nott   John Gamblin
    Rich Clarke   Geo Courtnell   Antho Linton

Robt Smyth his   250 acres due for transportation of the following
cert for Land   into the colony.
     Ann Smyth
     Sarah Smyth
     Rafe Gilbird
     Wm Stratford
     Mary Stratford

Mr Wright   "Whereas it appeareth unto the Court that Alice
agt   Atkinson hath in a most infamous manner defamed Mr
Alice Atkinson   Richd Wright in taxing him of Ravishm't and noe
                  proof thereof The Court doth therefore order that
the said Alice Atkinson shall have twenty stripes upon her bare
shoulders forthwith "

Note: Now please may I ask you, would the Father of His Country have
been so hard-hearted or have allowed any such situation to have arisen
in the first place ? My kindly and considerate reader knows very well
what I mean.   B.F.

Order Book #2.   20th August 1655.   page 33.

Mr Thomas his cert for Land	200 acres due to Wm Thomas assigned to Col. Mottram for transportation of following into colony.
	    Lydia Sayer
	    Edward Gover (Gower ?)
	    Thomas Glower
	    Lyonell Britton

A Report to the Governor and Council conc'r the proofs of Coll Mottroms Will	"To the Hon'bl Governor and Council Wee whose names are underwritten finding some ambiguities in the proving of Colonell John Mottrom decd his last will and Testament wee doe therefore refer the matter to y'r Hons'rs determination
	    Samuell Smyth
	    Will Nash
	    Hugh Lee
	    Richd Budd
	    John Rogers
	    Matth Rhodon "

Mr Lee agt Tho Kedby	Kedby owing Lee 500 lb. tobo. is ordered to pay by November 10th.
Wm Allen exempted from the Levies	"The Court doth order that de futuro William Allen shall be exempt from paying the County and Country Levies hee being above the age of sixty years "

Note: Therefore Wm. Allen was born circa 1595. B.F.

The next Court 20th 8thbr next	"It is ordered that the next Court to be held the 20th of 8th'er next at Mr Hugh Lee his house"

Note: In this eternal question of calculating the old time an easy way to remember the months is thus: September the 7th month, October the 8th, November the 9th and December the 10th. I wish they had not put 'th' after 22 and the above 'thbr' and 'ther' is even more than my long tongue can twist.   B.F.

Order Book #2. 22nd August 1655. page 33.

"August the 22th 1655
A list of the Vestry

For Chicacoan congregation
   Lieft Coll John Trussell : Mr Hugh Lee
   Capt John Rogers : Mr Matth Rhodon

For Cherry-point congregation
   Anthony Linton : George Nott

For Yeocomoco Congregation
   Mr Nicholas Jurnew : Jno Powell Church-Warden
   Richard Holden

For Wecocomoco Congregation
   Major Samuel Smyth : Mr James Hawley
   Jno Haynie : Edw Coales : Richd Spann Church Warden

For Chinckahan quarter
   Mr Wm Presly Church Warden
   Robert Newman : John Hull "

Order Book #2. 20th October 1655. page 33.

Mr Robert Burrell agt Wm Thomas	Order, dated 20th October 1655, that Thomas pay 300 lb. tobo. to Burrell "for the use of Mr. Wm Carver " Signed Nicholas Morris John Rogers

Order Book #2. 20th November 1655. page 33.

"Att a Court held for the County of Northumberland
   The 20th daye of November 1655
Present   Major Samuel Smyth   Capt Rich Budd
               Mr Hugh Lee   Capt John Rogers
               Mr Nicholas Morris   Mr Matth Rhodon   Com'rs "

Order for the Executor of Mr Nash to rec and pay debts	"The Court doth order that the Executor of the last will and Testament of Mr Wm Nash decd shall have the power to receive and pay debts x x the will being already proved untill Mris Nash her returne from her voyage from England or order from her "
Majo Smyth agt Mr Nich Morris Admr of Tho Coggin	"Whereas it doth appear unto me that Tho Coggin decd doth owe x x Major Samuell (Smith) the sume of 129 lb. tobo. x x ", Nicholas Morris, executor, is ordered to pay. Signed Hugh Lee.

Order Book #2   20th November 1655

Wm Presly
agt
Mr Nich Morris
Admr of Tho Coggin

Nich. Morris, Admr. of estate of Tho. Coggin, decd. ordered to pay 112 lb. tobo. to Wm Presly.

Abra Byram Exor
of John Foster
agt
Mr Nich Morris
Admr of Tho Coggin

Coggin owing Abraham Byram, Executor of John Foster, decd., 500 lb. tobo., Morris is ordered to pay from the estate

John Howell
agt
John Rawlings

Referred to next Court.

Order for Sarah
Kingwell to have
her bed and clothes

"The Court doth order that Sarah Kingwell widow and Relict of Thomas Kingwell decd shall have her bed and wearing apparell shee being left in a very sad condicon with a great charge of children "

Note: Avis Hickman may have arranged to paddle her own conoe but we will hold back our tears for the distressed Sarah for just a moment until we can read the entry to follow.   B.F.

Tho Garratt Admr
of Tho Kingwell

"The Court doth order that Tho Gerratt who marryed the widdow and Relict of Tho Kingwell decd shall have a Comisson of Admr of the Estate of the said Kingwell hee putting in an Inventory and security to the Court for the same "

John Baylor
agt
Robert Castleton

Robert Castleton acks. Judgmt. for paymt. of 1520 lb. tobo. to John Bayler. Signed Robert Castleton his marke.

Edward Henley
agt
Peircy Hammond

Hammond owing Henley 588 lb. tobo. is ordered to pay in ten days.

Order Book #2. 20th November 1655. page 34.

Mr Hugh Lee
agt
Tho Gerratt Admr
of Thomas Kingwell

Kingwell having owed Lee 325 lb tobo., Gerratt is ordered to pay.

Mr Nich Morris Admr
of Thos Coggin
agt
Tho Garratt Admr of
Tho Kingwell

Kingwell having owed Coggin 800 lb. tobo., Garratt is ordered to pay.

Order Book #2. November 1655. page 34.

John Johnson agt Tho Gerratt Admr Tho Kingwell	Kingwell having owed Johnson 383 lb. tobo., Garratt is ordered to pay.
Mr Hugh Lee agt Tho Gerratt Admr of Thomas Kingwell	Kingwell having owed Lee 325 lb. tobo., Gerratt is ordered to pay. (Note: This entry is in duplicate of that on page 65)
Robert Laud agt Richard Clare	Clare is ordered to return a canoe to Robert Laude.
Martin Cole agt Kingwells Estate	Cole to have 300 lb. tobo. for keeping Sarah the Relict of Thomas Kingwell eleven weeks.

Note: Martin Cole is yet another one who does not seem to measure up so remarkably well in the Virginia tradition, certainly not that of hospitality. The other creditors at least waited until Sarah could get herself another husband, at which sport, considering her sad state and many incumberances, she made pretty good speed.   B.F.

John Johnson agt Mr Morris Admr of Tho Coggin	Peter Knight petitions the Court in behalf of John Johnson for 590 lb. tobo., due from Coggin. Johnson having made oath before Mr James Hawley.
James Claughton Attr of ffrancis Jacob agt John Powell	Referred to next Court.
Henry Hurst to have possession of Land from Tho Kingwell	Kingwell having agreed to build some housing for Hurst for Land, and not doing it, the land ordered surrendered to Hurst.
Mr Newman agt Henry Cartwright	Cartwright owing Mr Robert Newman 480 lb tobo is ordered to pay.
Mrs Roberts agt John Powell	"Whereas Mrs Katherine Roberts was subpoened into the Court by John Powell for a witness agt James Claughton Atturney of ffrancis Jacobs" , Powell is ordered to pay her 20 lb. tobo.
Abraham Byram Executor of John Foster agt Martin Cole	Cole owing Foster 355 lb. tobo. is ordered to pay within ten days.

Order Book #2.   November 20th 1655.   page 34.

Mr Morris Admr of Tho Coggin agt Martin Cole	"Whereas it doth appear unto me that George Hale doth owe unto the Estate of Thos Coggin decd" 300 lb. tobo. "It is therefore ordered that Martin Cole who gave bond to the said Hale to save him harmlesse x x pay forthwith x x " Signed Samuell Smyth.
Martin Cole agt Mr Morris Admr of Tho Coggin	Coggin having owed Cole 82 lb. tobo. by Bill assigned from John Bennett, Morris is ordered to pay. Signed Samuell Smyth.
Mr Hugh Lee agt Mr Tho Broughton	Broughton ordered to pay Lee 600 lb tobo now in his hands and attached by Lee from estate of Wm Allenson.
Majr Sam Smyth agt Wm Spycer	"x x it doth appear x x that Wm Spycer doth owe unto Coll Wm Claiborne Esq " 332 lb. tobo., by bill to Major Samuel Smith from Spycer and Tho Prichett. The Court orders payment.
Mr Broughton agt Thomas Youle his Estate	Broughton to have Attachment agst. Est. of Thomas Youle, deceased, for 3600 lb. tobo. due by bill.
John Bayles agt Mr Robt Newman	To next Court at Mr Newman's request.
Wm Cornish agt Mr John Radford	To next Court at Mr Radford's request.

Order Book #2. 20th November 1655. page 35.

Abraham Byram Exor of John Foster agt John Bennett Exor of the said Foster	Bennett arrested and not appearing in suit of 4480 lb. tobo., is ordered to appear at next Court or order to pass agt. him for the debt.
Mr Peter Knight his motion	Regarding an action of debt betw. Knight and Col. John Mottrom, deceased.
Mr Wm Presly agt Mr Hugh Lee Admr of Robert Sharpe	Robert Sharpe, deceased, having owed Presly 165 lb. tobo. for Levies and Fees, Lee is ordered to pay from the estate.

Order Book #2. 20th November 1655. page 35.

Mr Broughton agt Mr Haukins	Mr Thomas Broughton to have attachment agt Estate of Mr Thomas Haukins for 328 lb. tobo. "as appears the amount by the corporall oath of the sd Mr Broughton in open Court and allsoe from under the hand of the sd Haukins his wife "
Wm Thomas agt Jno Gatehouse	Thomas to have attachment agt estate of John Gatehouse, 1203 lb. tobo. Debt having been ack. in Court by Col. Mottrom attorney for Gatehouse.
John Haynie his certificate conc Seating of Land	"These are to certify that according to the oathes of Robert Bradshawe and Thomas Hayle there were some trees felled and Peach trees planted on the Land of Mr Robert Newman being assigned to Jno Haynie which said trees were falne by the said Robt Bradshaur and Thos Hayle before the 25th of March in the year 1654 at the request of the said John Haynie "

Note: The question came up while making this transcript as to whether there were peach trees in Northumberland at so early a date. Yes there were. These trees matured rapidly. The peaches were made into brandy, which could be shipped ('on a shipp with a reliable commander' as one old letter said) and at that time had a good sale.   B.F.

Wm Presly agt Wm Allenson	Presly to have an attachment agst. the estate of Allenson "hee secretly depting out of this County" for 300 lb. tobo.
Machywax agt Coll Mottrom	"Whereas it doth appear unto the Court that Machywax the King of Chickacoan Indians delivered into the hands of Coll John Mottrom decd the quanity of one hundred arrmes length of Roanoke and noe account of the same given to the said King The Court doth therefore order the overseers of the sd Coll Mottrom shall within twenty dayes make paymt of the said Roanoke or such satisfaction as shall content the said Machywax out of the dec'ds Estate else Execution "
James Claughton agt John Powell	Claughton arrested and Powell not appearing against him, Powell is ordered to pay Claughton 50 lb. tobo
Wm Spycer agt Martin Cole	Referred to next Court at Cole's request.
Robert Lambden Constable for little Wicocomoco	"The Court doth order that Robert Lambden shall be Constable for Little Wicocomoco and hee further take his oath before a Comr.

Order Book #2. 20th Nov. 1655. page 35.

Richd Rayman agt Richd Gibble	Rayman arrested and Gibble not declareing against him is ordered to pay him 50 lb. tobo.
Mr Peter Knight agt Capt William Douglas and Company	Attachment on the estate of Capt. Wm Douglas & Co. to Knight for 5790 lb. tobo. now in his hands.

Wm Harding
his Censure
and Banishmt

"Whereas articles were Exhibited agt Wm Harding by mr David Lindsaye upon suspicion of Witchcraft Sorcery &c And an able Jury of Twenty fower men were impannelled to try the matter by verdict of woh Jury they found part of the Articles proved by severall depositions The Court doth therefore order that the said Wm Harding shall forthwith receive ten stripes upon his bare back and forever to be Banished this County and that hee depart within the space of two moneths And alsoe to paye all the charges of Court "

Note: The Rev. David hailed from a country where witchcraft and sorcery were not unknown in song, story and whispered family tradition. He doubtless knew it when he saw it. However his name appears in the record which is more than can be said for the brave twentyfour. It is a matter of great regret that I am unable to find any trace of these interesting depositions. Weighing every word in this entry, as well as those omitted, the thought occurs that had I been a first class, proven sorcerer, I would have called upon my friend the Devil, and with his help made it quite hot for this and that person in Northumberland before I departed the county within two months. And also, although I sedulously avoid murder trials in the press, passing funerals and other such heathenish manifestations, still I would just love to be able to step back to 1655, have been there, and been a part and parcel of this unholy adventure in the fourth dimension at the Northumberland Court.   B.F.

Mr Morris his Deede to Westgitt the Recording to be annuled	"Whereas there is recorded a writing or conveyance of Land from Mr Nicholas Morris to Adam Westgitt the 20th of August 1655 and not acknowledged in Court by the said Mr Morris The Court doth therefore order the said Recording shall be anehilated and anuled "
John Haynie agt Mr Cololough	George Cololough owing John Haynie 5750 six peny nayles, 500 single tens and 400 Double tens, and also two Bushells and halfe of salt, the Court orders that James Austen, Atturney of the said Mr Cololough, shal within 20 days, make payment.

Order Book #2. 20th November 1655. page 35.

Symon Richardson att of Tho Coniers agt Mr Morris	"Whereas x x Michael Brooke doth owe unto Thomas Coniers 5 Hhds of Tobo x x and whereas Wm Batten contrary to the Laue transported the said Brooks out of this colony and the said Batten being arrested to this Court att the suite of Symon

Richardson Att of the sd Coniers and neyther by himselfe nor his Atturney made appearance to the Court in defense x x ". Batten is ordered to appear at the next Court "That then Mr Nicholas Morris whoe was bound for the said Battens appearance shall x x make payment x of the x tobo x x to Simon Richardson Atturney for x x Coniers x x".

Abraham Byram Exor of John Foster agt John Bennett Exor of the sd Foster	Byram arrested and Bennett not appearing against him, Bennett is nonsuited and ordered to pay Byram 50 lb. tobo.
John Hull agt Daniell Holland and Joyce Holland	Referred to next Court at Hull's request.

page 36

George Courtnell agt Wm Little	Little ordered to pay Courtnell 500 lb. tobo.

page 36

John Hull in the behalf of his wife agt Joane Cornish	Referred to next Court at Hull's request.

page 36

John Haynie agt Seth Foster	Foster having arrested Haynie and not declaring against him, is nonsuited and ordered to pay him 50 lb. tobo.

page 36

Mr Wm Presly Collector for the Levie to have his Quietus est upon paymt of 1783 lb. of Tobo	"Whereas Mr Wm Presly was Collector for the Levys in the year 1654 x x" has presented his a/c to the Court, and paid excepting 874 lb. of tobo to Houell Price and 894 lb. tobo. to Capt John West, the Court orders that upon payment he to have Quietus est.

page 36.

John Haynie Clerke of the Markett att Wecocomoco	The Court orders that Mr. John Haynie shall be Clerk of the Market for great Wicocomoco and little Wicocomoco.

Order Book #2. 20th November 1655. page 36.

Church Wardens to destreyne for the Ministers Sallery	"The Court doth order that in case of non paymt every Church Warden within their Several Limmitts shall have power to destrayne for the ministers sallery it being fifty three pounds of tobacco and caske per poll "
Jane Owen agt Capt Ri Budd	"Whereas Jane Owen being the serv't of Capt Richard Budd made complaint unto this Court of abuse recd by her Mrs and whereas it doth appear by the oathes of Mrs Morris and Mrs Hawley that the said Jane Owen had about twelve markes black and blew about her The Court doth therefore order the sd Capt Budd shall further paye all the Charges of Court else Execution"
Lt Coll Jno Trussell to be Collector	"The Court doth order that Lieft Coll John Trussell High Sheriffe of Northumberland County shall be Collector for this yeares Levies "
Capt Jno Rogers and Mr Matth Rhoden	"Were sworne Com'rs before Coll John Mottrom about the latter end of May 1655"
Lieft Coll John Trussell	"Att the same time was sworne High Sheriffe of Northumberland County before Coll John Mottrom"

30 June 1655
"Capt Richard Budd was sworne a Commissioner "

Major Smyth his cert for Land	200 acres due for transportation of the following into the colony:
	    Elizabeth Reade
	    Bryand an Irishman
	    Tony a negro
	    Besse a negro

A Cert for the Rights of Land to Major Sam Smyth from Richd Bennett Esq	"These are to testifie that Mr Sam Smyth had of me one mayde servt the last yeare and one man servt this yeare for which the Land due for their transportation belongs to him Wittnes my hand the 20th of April 1654 Ri Bennett 20th November 1655 This writing was recorded"

Order Book #2.   20th November 1655.   page 36.

George Nott   "Wee being impannelled upon a Jury in a difference
agt   depending between George Nott pltf and Thomas
Thomas Philpott Philpott Defent concerning a Cowe delivered to John
               Kaye decd from James Willis decd the delivery of the
sd cowe being confest by the defdt - and the said Kaye dying before he
had performed more than halfe his service all the wages of the sd Kaye
considered Woe do Awarde x x the Defendt x x deliver to x x the Pltf
the x cowe The Pltf to pay Dfdt 170 lb tobo and all Charges of Court
x x x 20 November 1655"

    John Haynie   Henry Rooke   Edward Coles
    Ralph Horsley   Will Spycer   Geo Courtnell
    Abraham Byram   Symon Richardson   Robert Such
    Tho Broughton   John Parse   Dan Holland

Order for Mr Lee   "Att a Quarter Co'rt held at James Citty the 20
to be of the Quorum   October 1655". Present: Edward Digges, Esq.,
                      Governor, etc., Coll Wm Claiburne, Coll Tho
Pettus, Lt Coll. freeman, Coll Edward Hill, Esquires. Mr Hugh Lee is
ordered to be of the Quorum in the Commission of Northumberland
County, to take place next to those already in the Quorum. "Teste
Nich Meriwether Cl Con "

Order Book #2.   29th November 1655.   page 36.

"Att a Court held att the house of Mr Hugh Lee the 29th day of
November 1655"
Present   Major Sam Smyth   Capt John Rogers
            Mr Hugh Lee   Mr Matth Rhodon   Com'rs

Major Sam Smyth   Smyth to have cert. of admr. of the estate of
Ad'tor of Robt Duglas   Robert Duglas, decd.

Wm Thomas to have   Thomas to have the next order against the
next order agt the   estate of Duglas for 1000 lb. tobo.
Estate of Robt Duglas

Mr Hugh Lee   Lee to have judgmt. upon a bull of Allenson's
agt   estate.
Wm Allenson

Wm Presly   Presly to have judgmt for 300 lb. tobo. etc.
agt
Wm Allenson

            "Mr Lee drew up these orders "

Order Book #2. The following entries appearing on page 37 are out of order, appearing after those for the Court of 29th Nov. 1655, but each carries it's own date.

"Att a Co'rt held att the house of Collo John Mottrom decd the 30th daye of June 1655
Present   Mr Wm Nash   Mr Richd Budd
                Mr Jas Hauley   Mr Math Rhoden "

Mr Nich Morris   Morris to have cert. of Admr. on the estate of
Admr of   Tho. Coggin, decd.
Tho Coggin
              "20th 9ber 1655 This order was recorded"

Northumberland County, Virginia.
Record Book #14.

This book is badly mutilated. Where only fragments remain, my effort will be to show as much as I can of the original record. The entries begin in the year 1652.   Beverley Fleet.

Record Book #14. page 1.

John Hawkins   To Mr. Mottrom 800 lb. tobo. Refers to Mr. Wilsford.
his will   Out of the crop 300 lb. tobo. betwixt J- (prob.
                   John) Hawkins and Abraham Byram for land. More to
the parson out of the crop. Out of pigs upon the hill, three shares more to John Gresham. More to Thomas Kingwell. More from Abraham Byram to Thomas Kingwell. More to Henry Hurst from Jo- Ha- (prob. John Hawkins). The cow called - - betwixt Abraham and I, I give to Abraham B-. "I give to Thomas Byram one brown yearling with a starr in the forehead and if in case the boy dies the sd yearling with her increase to return to his father Abraham Byram." I give to Henry Hurst one cow. I give to Henry Moseley the younger one cow called Goldylox and a black heifer called Doll x x the first two cow calves they bring to his brother J- (prob. John) Mosely. If either of them should die x x. Their father to have the use of them till they come of age.   I give to Abraham Byram two brown heifers. I give the first cow calf to Helin Kingwell daughter of Thomas Kingwell.   I give to Abraham Byram the cow called Cherry and the Bull. "I give to Abraham Byram all my household goods and my gunn". I give Abraham Byram and Henry Moseley jointly the - due for the land at Kickata- at the Indian Spring n- (near) to ffoxhill. Likewise Abraham Byram to give to N- (prob. Nathaniel) Holling one cow calfe. " Witness my hand this fifth of ffebr 1651"
(1651/2)   Signed   John Hawkins.
Witnesses.
the Mark of N-iel Holling (prob. Nathaniel Holling)
Tho Kingwell
                             Recorded 20th September 1652.

Daniel Stepping   This entry mutilated. Half gone. Desires to be
his will   interred at the disposition of "my now present
                   friends." "And as for what estate I am now
possessed of in that present shipp called the Margott of London either in goods or in servants and likewise for goods or servants Bills Bonds or - - are either in my Brother Hugh fforshawes - or any other person or persons whatsoever in Virginia I wholly give and bequeath unto my welbeloved wife Elizabeth Stepping making of her full and whole executrix - - and further I doe make my wel beloved friends Mr Arthur Baly and Gyles Wright now aboard the shipp Margot overseers of this my will" Dated 13th day of - 1651.   Signed   Daniel Stepping.
Witnesses.
Edward Atwell
Thomas Hockin   (sic)
Thom- Young   Probated. 20th Sept. - -.

Record Book #14. page 2.

Tho Young his oath	"Thomas Young aged 24 yeares or thereabouts being sworne and examined saith That Daniel Stepping coming to Virginia in the good shipp called the Margaret of London" x x x "And he this Depon't with his - - Thomas Hawkins (sic) and Edward At- (Atwell) were witnesses". Entry mutilated, date, etc., missing. signed Tho Young.
Entry mutilated.	Evidently a patent of land issued to Lewis Burwell, Dated 17th October 1650. See next entry.

Record Book #14. page 3.

Mr Burwell his Assignment of the Pattent to Mr Turney	"Major Lewes Burwell of the County of Glouster" assigns his interest to Richard Turney. Dated 4th Sept. 1651. Witnessed by Th- Wilkinson. At the close of the entry "sign Leonard Go- ".
Mr Turney his assignm't of the Pattent to Mr Alderton Junr	Richard Turney assigns patent to Mr. Isaac Alderton, Junior. Dated 21st Sept. 1652. Witness, Jo Rosier.
John Walton his Pattent	Sir William Berkeley to John Walton, Cooper, land next to that of Nathaniel Pope, on the south side of the Potomac River, etc. Dated 3rd Sept. 165-. Entry badly mutilated.
John Walton his Assignment of the Pattent to Mr Jo Hollowes	Entry so badly mutilated that it cannot be read. The name Tho Wilsford appears and the date, 20th September 1652.
John Walton his Pattent	Sir William Berkeley to John Walton, 300 acres in Northumberland Co., on the east side of Hallowes Creek, adj. land of Mr. John Hallowes, due for the transportation of 6 persons, names not shown in record. Dated 15th September 1651.
John Walton his assignmt of the Pattent to Mr Hallowes	Walton assigns the foregoing to Mr. John Hallowes. Witnesses: John Handy, Tho Wilsford. Dated 20th September 1652.

Record Book #14. page 3.

John Essex his Pattent	Sir William Berkeley to John Essex, 500 acres in Northumberland Co., "abbutting on ffishing Creek" on south side of Great Wicocooomoco. Dated 30th - 1650.
Caption and half of entry gone.	Evidently an assignment of the foregoing. The name George Colclough appears, perhaps as a witness and the date, 20th September 1652.

Record Book #14. page 4.

Mr Burwell his lre of Attur to Mr Brodhurst	Power of Atty. from Lewis Burwell of Gloucester Co., to "Walter Brodhurst of Northumberland High Sheriffe " to collect debts. Dated 11th Dec. 16-. Witnesses: ffrancis Jarvis, the Mark of John -yor. Recorded 20th September 1652.
Miles Cooke his lre of Attur to Ralph Horsly	Power of Atty. from Miles Cooke to Ralph Horsly to collect debts due from Arthur Branch. Dated 15th March 1651 (1651/2). signed Miles Cooke. Witnesses: William Edwire, Rice Maddocke. Recorded 20th September 1652.
Mr Gerrard his lre of Attur to Mr Brodhurst	Power of Atty. Thomas Gerrard to Walter Brodhurst, dated 27th August - -. Recorded 20th Sept. 1652. Mutilated.
Caption mutilated.	Power of Atty. Richard Hawkins in the County of Northumberland, planter, to "my trusty and wel beloved friend Edward Thomson" to collect debts. Dated 17th Sept. 1652. Signed Richard Hawkins. Witness: The mark of John -quibb (Squibb) Recorded 20th Sept - - (1652).
Rich Hawkins his - of Attur to -gh Lee	Power of Atty. Richard Hawkins to "my trusty friend Hugh Lee" to collect debts from Thomas Hawkins in the County of Northumberland. Dated 18th September 1652. Signed "The Marke of Richard Hawkins". Witnesses: Tho Speke, Tho Youlle. Recorded 20th Sept. 1652.
Caption Mutilated.	Bill of Sale, Hugh Lee of Northumberland to Richard Hawkins "one blacke Cow wth a Browne lift right downe her backe" and other cattle. Dated 22nd Sept. 1651. Signed Hugh Lee. Witnesses: Tho Wilsford, Henry Rock. Recorded (appears to be) 14th June 1652.

78

Record Book #14. page 4.

Caption and entry mutilated.	Richard Hawkins assigns right in foregoing Bill to Tho. Hawkins. Date missing. Signed Richard Hawkins his marke. Witness: Hugh - -. Recorded 20th September - -.
Caption and entry mutilated.	"The Deposition of Edward Thomson aged 36" relative to delivery of cattle in the transaction between Tho. Hawkins, Richard Hawkins and his wife (her name not shown) and Hugh Lee whose home was at Chicacone. Signed by Edward Thomson and sworn in Court 20th September 1652.

Record Book #14. page 5.

Isaac Knight his Deposition	Regarding the foregoing. Signed "per me Isaack Knight thirty yeares old 17th Septem 1652". Sworn before Tho Speke.
Geo Thomson and Hen Cartwright their Bill to John Dandy	Entry mutilated. Thompson and Cartwright to John Dandy and Thomas Maidwell. Dated 3rd July - -. Witness: Tho Philpot his mark. Recorded 20th September 1652.
James Claughton his Deposition	"James Claughton aged 23 yeares or thereabouts" regarding hogs and supplies bought by him from John Earle. A part of this property sold by Earle to Henry Haler and a pig to Wm. Bedlam. Signed by James Claughton and sworn to 20th Sept. 1652.
John Ingrams receipt for 18 hhds of Tobaco of Thomas Hawkins	Ingram promises to deliver aboard the Margaret of London. Dated 5th March 1651 (1651/2) Signed John Ingram. Witness John Dennes.
Tho Hawkins his -ccons to Jon -gram	"A note of direccion what you have to doe And if yow goe aboard of Mr Baily bring up the hhead of malt and the shott and old clothes and the rest of all my things and my leaden weight and remember me to all the Company".
Ingrams Accot Tho Hawkins	"Mr Tho Hawkins Debtr To bring his Tobco from Hampton River to Capt Batts ffor three men two Dayes about the Tobco To going to Virginia for evidences " Signed John Ingram, and sworn in Court 20th Sept. 1652.

Record Book #14. page 5.

-- Batte his receit Receipt of William Batte to John Ingram for 18
-- hheads of - -   hhd. of tobo. for Thos Hawkins. Dated 13th March
of Jo Ingram   1651 (1651/2). This name may well be Balle or
                  Bailey, since frequently the double lls are
                  crossed in this hand as though they were double
                  tts.

Caption   William Batte (possibly Bailey) certifies that
mutilated.   Thos Hawkins has disposed of the tobacco that John
                  Ingram left at Buckrowe and sent a letter to Capt.
Whitty to take the remainder and carry it home to one Capt. Jordan, and
that Capt. Whitty had given order to see if it is marketable. Dated - -
August 1652.

Record Book #14. page 6.

William Parry   "The Deposition of William Parry saith That - - at
his Deposition   the house of Capt Batt in the company of Thomas - -
                  the Depont going for a hhead of Tobco and went into
- - - where Thomas Hawkins was looking over some - - and the said Hawkins said that he would make John I- - pay for the damages of his Tobco
whereupon Thom- - - desired your Depon to looke upon the said Tobaco
and - - it were damnified in the boate or rotten before whor- your
depont tooke out a handfull of the said Tobaco and - - it was rotten
before and put it up in his handkercher - - carried it home and further
saith not   William P- - his marke". Age not shown in deposition.

Note: William may not have known how to write, but at least he had a
hankerchief, an elegant detail when one considers how noses were
usually blown in those days.   B. F.

John Sheppard   Deposition sworn to 19th August 1652. "That about
his Deposition   May last hee came down with John Ingram from
                  Chickacone in a shallop x x x and saith that from
the setting out from the harbor from Chickacone to their casting anchor
in Hampton River there fell no rain neither was there any bulge (sic)
water in the boate that he conceiveth could doe the Tobaco any harme
The said Ingram imploying a Boy that came with him belonging to the said
Hawkins to throw out the water when there was any and further saith not"
Signed John Sheppard. "Teste me Henrico Poole". Age not shown in deposition.

Ralph Horslys   "Ralph Horsly aged 42 yeares or thereabouts". Re-
Deposicon   garding Ingram delivering the tobacco to Batte and
                  being thanked by Thomas Hawkins. Dated 20th Sept.
                  1652. Signed Ralph Horsly his marke.

Record Book #14. page 6.

Jane Horsly her Attestacon

This entry mutilated. Margin of page torn away. " x x Jane Horsly aged 40 yeares" says she heard "Thos Hawkins also Jonathan Stepping to go - - - but being sicke he would not goe Haw- - - replyde it was best for him to goe to his sister - - - - after the wife of the said Hawkins came to this Att- - weeping and said her husband would have Jo- - - - his sister The said Attestant answeared - - - he should be forced to goe to his sister -.- - would give him his Dyett till he was well which - - - done for this 7 weeks In witnes of the truth she - - subscribed her hand the 21st of Septem: 1652". Signed Ja- Horsly her Marke. Witnesses: John Dandy his Marke, Tho Broughton.

Caption destroyed.

"The estate of John Warre decd Debtor 1651" Items include "Re'd from John Haney 120 tobo", "paid Mr ffoster Mr Presleys order 188 lb. tobo." "Jurat Coram me Jo Mottrom". "The marke of Robt Newman", "28th Sept 1652 This accot was Recorded".

Mr Phillips his receit of a Prisoner from Mr Smith

"These may cert- whom it may concerne that on the 27th of Septem: I receaved of Mr Samuel Smith Sherr of Northumberland a Prisoner John Newman apprehended upon suspicon of Murther and Comitted unto the Custody of the said Mr Sa Smith by a Writt under the hand of Mr Geo ffletcher to be conveyed to James Citty Dated the day and yeare above written   John Phillips
9 Octo 1652 This was Recorded"

Jane Perry her will

The will of Jane Perie. "My body to be decently buried by my husband Pery."   To my daughter Jane "one great brass kettle" and other personal property, including all wearing apparel.   "To my daughter Margarett" personal property.   To "my daughter Elizabeth" personal property including a frying pan at Richard Span's house, one bible and Practice of Piety at John Powell's house.   "To my son -" page mutilated here, appears to be William, two heifers, a looking glass and a pestle. "I give to my son Andrew one black cow one little gunn and if I dye this sickness my will is that this boy Andrew shal be bound Apprentice to Hugh Lee for eight years he to teach him to reade and write and to give him at the end of his time two suites of apparrell and a cow calfe".   Certain property to be sold and debts and funeral charges paid. Half of the balance to daughter Elizabeth and the other half to daughters Jane and Margarett.   Overseers "my loving friends - - - Allenson and Ralph Horsly and Hugh Lee". Dated 4th ffebruary 1650. (1650/1)   Signed   Jane Pery her Marke.
Witnesses:
William Allenson his Marke
Richard White his Marke
Hugh Lee   Probated 20th May 1651.

Record Book #14.   page 7.

Jane Perye — "A true and Just Inventory of the Goods and
her Inventory   Chattles of Jane Pery deceased taken the 3 of
                 March 1650" (1650/1).
This inventory includes:
One plantacon 200 Acres of Land
One looking glass three bibles and one Practice of Piety
One pair of old silk stockings one pair of greene stockings
x x fowre old pictures
one black taffaty neck cloth   etc. etc.
Signed: Wm Reynolds, Tho Keene, Phill Carpenter, ffran Simons.

Note: In and among these colonial inventories appear certain items
that cannot but arouse interest if one has the least sentiment. Here
are four old pictures in 1651. Were these just four dirty old pictures
or were they four quaint old Perry family portraits ?   B. F.

"An Inventory of the Goods of Walter Danell deceased" appraised by
John Dennis, John Gamlin and John Larrett. "sworne and appointed the
first day of Novem: 1650". The total amounts to 350 lb. tobo. Then
there is this note: "A Bundle of writings left in the office wch did
belong to Walter Danell wch the Administrator will not meddle with
but is lawfull for any Creditor of the deceased to take them by
Order of Court".

Note: Well I can tell you that I would meddle with them if I had
half a chance at this late date and I have an idea that Mr. Charles
B. Heinemann of Chicago, the authority on the Virginia Daniel family,
would come right on by plane if he were informed that they were
available.   B. F.

"Cornelius Robinson his Acco of Walt Danell estate
    Impremis paid John Gresham   400 and Caske
    Item   paid Mr Mottrom   250 "   "
    Item   paid Mr Speke   600 "   "
           Wm Bedlam   155 "   "
           Ralph Horsly   375 "   "
                                        - - - -
                                        1780

Note: At times it is difficult to decide just what these names may
be. The name shown above as Danell may possibly be Dauell therefore
even Davell, all of which opens up one of those petty arguments that
annoy and leave one uncertain.   B.F.

(Daniel-Dowell-deVille- -, Devil.)

Record Book #14.   page 7.

Wm Reynolds his   "A true and Just Accompt of the estate of James
Accot of James   Claughton deceased presented to the Court holden
Claughtons estate   at Northumberland by his Ma'ties Comiss'rs at the
                       house of Mr John Mottrom the 20th of August 1648
by William Reynolds Administrator of the said estate". The total value
of the estate was 3905 lb. tobacco and includes the following items:
"paid to Capt Claiborne by Ord'r from James Citty one heifer at   650
  To the hire of Indian   70
  More for a passage in Knifes and Rhonoake   35
  paid Hugh Lee for writing   100
  Mr Trussell by Order   150
  Mr George Higgins per order John Hampton   100
  Mr Wilkinson per order   350
  Mr Richard Thompson per Order 20 armslength of Rhonoake   "

Record Book #14.   page 8.

James Claughton   Presented to the Court - April 1647.
his Inventory   This inventory includes the items listed below.

"One old sattin petteecoat two black hoods one maske one paire
    of stockins one black neckcloth and a small parcell of
    lace"   150
one Taffatye petticot   160
Three books   10
One Wainscott Chest   40
etc. etc.   ----
                           Total   3536
Signed
    Geo Higgins   Wm Hardich
    Jo Handy   Tho - -
    Matt Rhoden   Prisers.

Note: The comparative value of the three books shows the high vener-
ation for learning held by the 'Prisers'.   B.F.

James Claughton's inventory continued.
August 3rd 1647.
"Thomas Brodnax of the Isle of Kent his Bill   1200
 Thomas Hayles by Bill   365
 Nicholas Pichard by Bill   400
 John Gresham by Bill   700
 John Gresham one Bill more   300
 Thomas Gam-s by Bill 30 shillings sterling
 Mr Wm Bran-le by Bill   300
19 August 1651 This Inventory was Recorded "

Record Book #14. page 8.

"Mr Hallowes Acco of Jo Hamptons Estate
    John Hamptons Acco Debtor"
The total of the account is 6370 lb. tobo. The following items are included:

```
"  Item  paid to Wm Hardish              220
   It    paid to Mr Chaddock              60
   It    paid to Henry Brooks            100
         paid Mr Hiller
   It paid to Mr Brackett                304
   It    paid to Michael Tainter         100
   It    paid to Wm Cocke                160
   It    paid to Nathaniel Jones          70
   It    paid to Mr Lord                 350
   It    paid to Mr Speke                285
   It    paid ffrancis Gray wch he
         receaved by Ord'r of Court      560 "
```
No date shown in this entry.

Caption worn away.
"An Inventory of the Goods of Mr William Nicholls late whilest he lived at Chickacone in the County of Northumberland in the Colony of Virginia deceased taken and appraised the 6th of May 1651 by John Haney and James Macgregger appointed and sworne by Mr Willm Presly". Page mutilated. Items listed include:

```
"Inprs  6 Books                            60
   Itm  a Barbers Case a Rasor Sysers glass
        and combe                          30
   Itm  there is a Bill of Thomas Bacons of
        Kicougha- x x "
```


Record Book #14. page 9.

Mr Winter Chapman his Inventory

"An Inventory of certain Goods of Mr Winter C- - - deceased". Total 1145 lb. tobo.
Signed Wm Hardich   Tho Youlle
    Zeph: Smith   Edw Thompson
Dated March 22nd 1650   (1650/1)

Mr Hallowes his Acco of Mr Sedgraves estate

"The Accompt of Mr John Hallowes Administrator of all and singulor the Goods and Chattles of Mr Robert Sedgrave late whilest he lived in the County of Northumberland in the Colony of Virginia deceased taken the 20th of Septem 1651 ". Items listed include:

```
Impr :paid and laid out to Jo Biscoe   Itm paid to Mr Pope
Itm paid Mr Chaddocke                  Itm paid to Capt Baldridge
Itm paid Capt Hill for him             Itm paid to Mr Hiller
Itm paid Capt Poythers                 Itm paid to Wm Hardich
Itm paid Mr Speke
```
    Total of account 3844 lb. tobo.

Record Book #14. page 9.

George Higgins Will of George Higgins. Dated 27th of Novem.1648.
his will "My loving friend Mr John Trussell of Northumberland in Virginia" sole Executor. To Thomas
Hales "half my shallop" and also cattle. To Robert Huinbourne cattle
and certificate for 300 acres of land. To Thomas Jelles the younger
"my Godsone in Virginia my little birding peice". After four years,
Exor. to give to Samuel Lonng and John Hayles son of Thomas Hayles, each
of them a cow calfe. If one of the aforesaid children die before he
comes of age, the other to have both calves.
    Witnesses John Pites   signed   George Higgins.
               Hugh Lee
                        Probated 20th September 1651.

Elizabeth Bedlam   "Elizabeth Bedlam aged 30 years or thereabouts
her deposition   sworne and examined" makes a statement regarding a
                  slight change in George Higgin's will, according to
                  his request, relative to the bequest to Mr John
                  Trussell.

Record Book #14. page 10.

Rich White his   Richard White of Northumberland, Carpenter, sells
sale of a gun to   a gun to Kelly. Dated 22nd Oct. 1652.
John Kelly   Signed Richard White his marke
                     Witnesses: Tho Wilsford, Henry Toppin.
                     Recorded 22nd October 1652.

Tho Hailes   Thomas Hailes of Youocomoco in the County of
his marke   Northumberland and Colony of Virginia, planter,
                     registers mark for hogs. Dated and recorded 23rd
                     October 1652.

Mr Pitt his lre   Power of Atty., Robert Pitt of the Isle of Wight
of Att to Jo Pitt   Countie, merchant, to "my sone John Pitt" to
                     receive 2800 lb. tobo. from Hugh Lee. Dated 29th
                     May 1650.   signed Robert Pitt.
                     Witnesses: Hen Pitt, William Dawson.
                     Recorded 25th October 1652.

John Pitt his   Power of Attorney. John Pitt, attorney for his
lre of Attur to   father Robert Pitt, appoints "my loving friend
Wm Thomas   William Thomas" attorney to receive 2800 lb. tobo.
                     from Hugh Lee. Dated 4th March 1651 (1651/2).
                                       signed   John Pitt.
                     Witnesses: Jane Packer, Boardit Peirce.
                     Recorded 25th October 165- -.

Record Book #14. page 10.

Mutilated.
Caption gone.

"Attestacon of Elinor Dorrill aged 37 yeares or thereabouts sworne saith That she heard Simon Richardson sweare that he would revenge himselfe on Wm Thomas and he desired yo'r Deponent to tell Edward Coles wife that the said Thomas tolle him that he had had the carnall or familiar use of her and would have it again in spight of her husbands teeth or any other mans And the said Richardson brought a Clubb in his hand into yo'r deponents house and threatened the said Thomas wheresoever he mett him and the said Thomas boy coming unto yo'r Depont the said Richardson told him that he would fight with his master wheresoever he mett him and further saith that the said Richardson came unto yo'r Depon't and would have given me a Heifer if that I would have defamed Mrs Coles She being a woman by whom I never saw any incivillity or dishonesty in word or deed and I answered him that I would not nor could not doe such an unjust action And as for the said Thomas I never heard him say nor know that he had the familiar or carnall use of Mrs Coles or any other woman whatsoever ffurther saith not Signum Ellinor Dorrill   Jurat Coram me Nicholas Morris
Recorded this Attestacon the 20th Septem: 1652 ".

Tho Dorrill
his Attestacon

"The Attestacon of Thomas Dorrill aged 33 yeares or thereabouts sworne saith That Simon Richardson coming at my house Wm Thomas came in about some business to me and the said Richardson began to rangle with the said Thomas and after the said Thomas was gon your Depon't heard the said Richardson say that Wm Thomas told him at that time that he had had the familiar use or that he had swifed Edward Coles wife and would swife her againe in spight of her husband or any other man And further your Depon't testifieth that he never heard any such words from Wm Thomas neither by Edward Coles wife nor any other woman whatsoever at that time or at any other time nor never knew any dishonest act by the man neither in that way or any other way ffurther saith not Signum Thomas Dorrill   Jurat Coram me Nicholas Morris
Recorded this Attestacon the 20th Sept 1652 ".

Caption
Missing

William Betts and Mary Purnell discharged from paying Bill by which they are bound to Tho Stevens.
Witnesses: Signed   Marke of Mary Purnell
Woodhall Street
Edward Coles
"This Discharge Recorded 10 Nov 1652".

Record Book #14. page 11.

Tho Broughton
his Deposicon

"Thomas Broughton aged 29 yeares or thereabouts sworne and examined saith" that the past April with Wm Reynolds, Ralph Horsly and George Co- -, he was requested to appraise the estate of Daniel S- - deceased. That William Reynolds purchased a pair of curtains, valued at 100 lb. tobo, at the appraisal from Thomas Hawkins, etc.   Signed Tho Broughton.
"Jurat in Cur 20 Sept 1652".

Ralph Horsly
his Deposition

"Ralph Horsley aged 42 yeares or thereabouts deposeth upon oath" that Wm Reynolds bought a suite of Curtains of Thomas Hawkins for 100 lb. of tobo., and that they were delivered. Signed Ralph Horsly his mark.
"Jurat in Cur 20 Sept 1652".

Wm Willday
his Deposition

"Wm Wildey aged 38 yeares or thereabouts being sworne and examined saith That Christopher Willance desired this Depon't to speake to Richard Span to to provide him his hhead of Tobco against he came up And further This Depon't saith not   William Willday   Jurat in Cur 25 Nevem: 1652"

Corbet Podle his marke of hoggs and Cattle

Mark registered 25th November 1652.

Wm Spicer
his Deposicon

"Wm Spicer aged 38 yeares or thereabouts saith That he heard Thomas Cogg- (page mutilated) John Essex his plantacon that he had bid John Gresham take his cowe againe ffurther this Depont saith not Signum Wm Spicer
Jurat - - - Septem: 1652 Coram John Mottrom   Recorded this Depo: 25th Novem: 1652 ".

Caption destroyed.

" I on a day coming unto John Essexs house Thomas Coggin being there and other Company I asked him to sell me the Cowe wch was once mine Hee answered me that she was none of his I asked whose she was then and he said John Gresham had her againe I asked him how that came to pass he told me he could not pay him his Tobco for them   Tho Kingwell "
Sworn in Court 26th November 1652.

Record Book #14. page 11.

Caption torn away.

"To his approved loveing friend Mr Nathaniel Pope at Appomattacks in Virginia

Loveing freind Mr Pope   I kindly salute you with hope of your health as I bless God I am at this present Sr I writt you severall lres that I had sent you some goods in Mr Webber by the way of New-England and that I would send you a good Cargo of goods by my man Richard Nicholls and I sent another by another servant of myne named Benjamin Stoane you have heard I know of the casting away of Mr Webbers shipp in the coast of New-England and since that I have heard of the death of my servant Benjamin Stone but thanks be to God I heard that Richard Nichols is safe arrived but I have not as yet received any letters from him since that he came into your parts but what I have by some that came from thence that wee have 15 saile of shipps that came about 14 dayes since into Portsmouth but are not as yet come into our Downes I haveing not as yet rec'd any lre from Rich: Nicholls causeth me to feare that all is not well with him but however I hope the best I desire the Lord to preserve him I know that he hath soe much business on his hands by reason of Bens: death that it seemeth to me something difficult for him to goe through without the assistance of some friend I hope that you have given him your best assistance and I hope that you and the rest that I deale with all did keepe your Tobco for Richard Nicholls as I did desire you and them to doe in my former letters and Mr Webber the wch lres I hope you have received by Mr Thurstons shipp Sr I did desire you to assist my servant as much as you would and I could and would serve you here Sr I have sent you in Mr Butlers a young man the wch I would desire you to take into your house and let him have meate and drinke and lodging and to imploy him in the best imployments that you shall see him capable of I conceave that he wil be fitt to teach your Children for he can write a very good hand sifer very well and is able to keepe your Accots if you conseave it meete Sr I would desire you to take him till such time as you shall heare from me wch shal be by the next shipping God willing his name is Samuel Mottershed I hope that my man hath made bold to have you overseer of my debts he hath left in the Country I would desire you to take care of it and to receive it into your custody for my use and I will give you content for your care and paines and you shall find me willing to serve you here in England your brother hath sent you a lre by the young man named Sam: Mottershed your father is well also Thus in haste I comitt you to the protecon of the Almighty and rest your loveing freind in all hearty love and affeccon to serve - "

Signed   Ni- - - -ayward.
Nicholas Hayward

Recorded - - - 25th Novem: 1652.
Bottom of page mutilated.

Record Book #14. page 12.

Mr Haywards lre of Attur to Rich Nicholls

Nicholas Hayward of London, merchant, to Richard Nicholls, to transact business in Virginia and Maryland. Refers to "Richard Nicholl my trusty servant". Dated 27th Sept. 1651.

Signed Nicholas Hayward.

Witnesses:
Richard Husband
- - Cowell
Ben Stone   (Page mutilated)

Record Book #14.   page 12.

Rich Nicolls   Rich Nicholls, Attorney for Nicholas Hayward, to
Assigmt to   Nathaniel Pope to transact business in Virginia.
Mr Pope   Dated 25th July 1652.   Signed Rich Nicoll.
                        Witnesses: David Anderson, Alex Baincham.
                        Recorded 25th November 1652.

Caption   "I Samuel Mottershed aged 22 yeares or thereabouts
Mutilated   sworne and examined saith That Mr Nicholas Hayward
                        comeing downe to Gravsend came aboard in the morning and tooke me ashore and after some discourse pul'd out a l're and woud have given it me but took a for-thinking and said he would take it backe lest he should have something more to write and said he would send it me more he bad me at our parting to remember him to Mr Pope and tell him that if his man Richard Nicholls were dead or coming into England that he would receave his Tobco that were in debts and he would give him content and more to desire him to speake to his Customers to keepe their Tobco for him And further saith not".
                                         Signed   Samuell Mottershed
"Jurat in Cur 25 Novem 1652"

Note: Now just a moment to sifer and for-thinking. This young gentleman stands up in Court and swears that his name is Samuel Mottershed. I doubt it. Times were bad at home for aristocrats. Why was the careful and important Mr Hayward so anxious that this young man be well taken care of ? Why was it necessary to take him ashore for last instructions instead of having that conversation on the ship ? Whence the old English appearing in the deposition ? That spoken English we know so well from the Council Group of the past. Shades of the old elegance rise before me.   Bev. Fleet.

- - Baker   "The deposition of Thomas Baker aged 26 or there-
- - Deposition   abouts being sworne saith That being by accident
                        at ffrancis Grayes there being ffrancis Gray and
Mr Hampton heareing Mr Hampton say to ffrancis Gray Gossip Gray I have lived with you a long time you never gave me anything what will you give ffrancis Gray replying I will give you a heifer calfe Mr Hampton giveing him thanks saying soe freely as you give it me I will give it to your sone Joshua ffurther the Depont saith he was coming at an other time from Thomas Boyds to ffran Grays house at goodwife ffoords plantacon heareing Mr Hampton say this is the Calfe that I gave to my Godson Joshua ffurther saith not Tho Baker his mke   Sworne before me Tho Baldridge Record 25 Novem 1652 ".

John Walker his   John Walker of Youocomoco sells Richard Holden of
sale of Land to   the same place, 450 acres of land called Youocomoco
Richard Holden   necke. Dated 24 Novem: 1652.
                                 Signed The marke of John Walker.
                        Witnesses: Tho Speke, ffran Gray.
                        Recorded 25th November 1652.

89

Record Book #14. page 13.

Nathaniel Jones   Entry mutilated. "Novem: the 22th 1652"
his Deposicon   "Nathaniel Jones aged 24 yeares or thereabouts sworne and examined saith That he heard Thomas Baker and - - Knight both say unto him in the time that Thomas B- - and Thomas Knight did live upon the plantacon wch - - John Hillers that then this Depon't heard Tho Baker - - being in discourse concerning a Boare of Mr John Ham- deceased Tho Baker replyed saying faith the Boare - - my dogg and I killd the Boare and this depon't saith - - Tho Knight confessed the same being at that time both - - Copartners in the estates and also this Depon't saith Th- said Baker and Knight said they did bury the same - - within the plantacon and further this Depon't saith - (not) The Marke of Nathaniel Jones Taken before Mr Nath Pope and Major Tho Baldridge Recorded the 25th Novem 1652".

Note: We wonder what the civilized Mr. Mottershed thought of this incident. Important or not, here is what happened. These razor-backed boars ranging through the Virginia woods are meaner than the Devil. Tom Baker's dog set on the boar. The boar set on the dog and was getting the best of it when Tom arrived to the rescue. The boar was more or less decently buried (perhaps) by Messrs Baker and Knight, who foolishly hoped they would hear no more of the matter. B.F.

Robert Hennibourne   "December the ffith 1651 A true and just Inventory
his Inventory   of the estate of Robert Hennibourne deceased -"
Total 2626 lb. tobo.
"Appraised by us   John Powell his marke
                James Claughton "

Caption torn away.   "The Accompt of Tho Hailes Administrator of all and singular the Goods Rights and Creditts of Robert Hennebourne late whilst he lived of Youocomocoe in the County of Northumberland and Colony of Virginia deceased Taken allowed of the 25th of Novem 1652". Total 2723 lb. tobo. Items include:

Itm paid Henry Haler (Hailes) for worke about getting in and houseing the deceaseds Cropp	050
Itm paid Wm Bedlams wife for washing the deceaseds Linnen in his life time	050
Itm paid Mr Hollowes x x due by the deceased	391
Itm paid Hugh Lee by Order of this Court	315
Itm paid John Haney for a debt due by the deceased	300
Item paid Mr Maddox for Phisicke for the deceased	060
Itm paid to Mr Speke x x for debt	343
Itm Paid to Colonel Mottrom for goods which were delivered for the use of the deceased though lost by Wm Jackson	186
Itm paid for the Caske of Mr Speke and Jo: Haneys Tobco being two hheads	050
Itm paid to John Powell and James Claughton for praising the estate of the deceased	200

Dated 25th Nov. 1652. Signed George Colclough, John Haney.
Recorded 25th - - 1652.

Note: So a hhd. was worth 25 lb. tobo. (3 books 10 lb. tobo.). Considering the fact, Mr. Maddox was overpaid. We hope Jackson's conscience hurt him, but we doubt if it did.   B.F.

Record Book #14.   page 14.

Walter Allenson his Indenture to Walter Weekes	Indenture 26th Nov. 1652, betw. Walter Weekes of Cherry-point in Northumberland and William Allenson of the same place. "Wm Allenson hath putt out - Walter Allenson his sone an Apprentice unto the said

Walter Weekes" for 15 years. To be taught "to reade English soe soone as he shall be capable of teaching". Does not state Weeke's business or trade. Signed Wm Allenson. Witnesses: Johis Kent, Peircy Hamon, Tho Wilsford.   Recorded 27th Nov. 1652.

Humfrey ffulford his sale of Cattle to John Raven	Humfrey ffulford of Chicacone in Northumberland, planter, sells to Raven "two head of neate Cattle". Dated 24 Oct. 1652. Signed Humfrey ffulford his Marke. Witnesses: The marke of Hugh ffouch, Jeremy Allam, John Hainey. Rec. 25th Nov. 1652.
- - Mottrom his - - of a Cowe - -h White	John Mottrom of the County of Northumberland, gent., sells a cow to Richard White. Dated 24th May 1651. Signed John Mottrom. Witness John Bennett.
Rich White his Assignmt of a Cow to Tho Wilsford	28th Decem: 1652. The above cow assigned to Wilsford. Signed Richard White his marke. Witnesses: Ralph Horsly his marke, Hen Rayner. Rec. 28 Dec. 1652.
- - Burwell his - Mr Brodhurst	"ffor his respected ffriend Mr Walter Brodhurst at his house upon Nominye Potomacke River present".

"Mr Brodhurst   And my most hon'd friend Yo'rs: I rec'd wherein I understand yo'r great care always of yo'r absent friend wch I hope shall not dye unrequited if I survive this my long sickness wch hath bene of a yeares continuance what you have or shall receive I shall desire you to convey to me as soone as possible but if you valleu your friend buy your young sone with a Cowe with part of it or else you injure me   The porke and Corne canot come in more welcome time   some troubles I have undergone in these change of time but God hath delivered me out of them   I shal be still ready to manifest that friendship wch I have at all times pretended and be ready to assist you in any thing that lyes in my power   By the next I shall inlarge wch at this time I canot being ill and unsettled in minde   My respect to yourself and good wife   I am Mr Brodhurst that friend wch truly loves and respects you and shall doe whilest I am
Octo the 12th 52   Lewis Burwell "
                       Recorded the - - - 1652.

Record Book #14.   page 15.

Mr Robert Atkinson his will	Page mutilated. The will of Robert Atkinson. Exor. Mr Billingsby. To Simon Oversea an - - for my last Cargoe of goods. "I desire also Mr Billingsby for

to give satisfaction to Mr Corbet Pydell Chyrurgion of Charges for his care and meanes that he hath done me I desire Mr Billingsby for to convey all the rest of my estate to my father and Mother to Hollan (sic) at the next shipping eavry one being satisfied". Dated 21 July 1652.
Witnesses: Signed Robert Atkinson.
Henry Brooke his marke, Phillip Silvester.
Will Proved in Court 20th.Janu 1652. (1652/3)

Record Book #14. page 15.

Phill Silvester his Depo	"The Deposition of Phillip Silvester aged 30 yeares or thereabouts on the 17th day of Janu: 1652 Saith That Corbet Fydle sending for him to his house

where being come a man a Duchman lyeing sicke upon his bed woh requested him for to wright his will and Testament wch the said Phillip Silvester did write by the said Duchmans Ord'r and but of his owne proper mouth and that the said will writt by the abovesaid Phillip Silvester was truly writt according to the Duchmans appointm't and direccons   Phillip Silvester   Taken before me Tho Baldridge"
                    "Recorded the 20th of Janu 1652" (1652/3)

Hen Rocke his sale to Jo Rocke	Henry Rocke sells cattle to John Rocke. This page is mutilated. Apparently the increase of this cattle to go to the son of John Rocke, at that time

a child. Although it may be that John Rocke is himself the child mentioned. Dated 19 January 1652 (1652/3) Signed Henry Rocke. Witnesses: Cyprian Bishop his marke, David Spiller his marke, Hugh Lee.   Recorded 20th Janu: 1652. (1652/3)

Caption mutilated.	Page badly stained. "In the name of God Amen know all men that I Thomas Keene being fresh of memory doth as followeth ffirst I bequeath my spiritt to

God that gave it after my body to the earth and then as followeth I give and bequeath to my sone Thomas one Cowe named Cole   next to my Daughter Susana one Heifer called by the name of Su   next I give my sone William one heifer named Gentle   next I give my sone Matthew the next Cowe Calfe that falleth of the old Cowes

Matthew Rhodon oweth me for a 11 hheads and 18 pounds since the last yeare	293
Mr Lee oweth me of amidst this yeare for six hheads & a paile	180
Richard Walker paid Mr Wilsford for my use	029
for hooping two pailes for Mr Wilford (sic)	030
to Mr Wilford for two hheads	050
for a Barrell to Mr Wilford	030
Richard White oweth me for a quarter of Beefe	200
Richard White for a hhead	025
Phillip Carpenter for 3 hheads	075
Phillip Carpenter for a churne	060
Henry Moseley upon Accot this yeare	150
Wm Medcalfe upon Accot last yeare	095
Henry Rainer for Caske washing and a paile	555
In Mr Mottroms hands	040
Simon Richardson for Court charges	080
John Gresham upon an Ord'r of Court	213
Mr Lee signed over fifty for my use Gresham to pay	050
Paid for Greshams use to Ralph Horsly	035
Upon debts when wee Reckned upon John Greshams Accots Debtor	330
Mr Colclough	092
George Courtnall oweth	155
Ralph Horsly oweth me for a quarter of Beefe this yeare	200
Ralph Horsly oweth me for 2 hheads	050
Ralph Horsly for a paile and a Churne	080

(continued on page 92)

Record Book #14. page 15.

The will of Thomas Keene continued.

Ralph Horsly accot and myne of last yeare stands one about another in a little booke of his	000
ffrancis Simons oweth me	048
Wm Reynolds	040
John Bennett	070

	3305

    Know all men that I doe give to my wife Mary Keene for the bringing up of my children all my moveable goods and hoggs and cattle but what I have given to my children and the remainder of my Tobco when my debts is paid is to my wife Also I give this land and plantacon to my wife during her life after her decease I give the said land to my sone Tho: and his heirs forever. Overseers of the estate Hen Mosely John Stanly Thomas Orlye (Hawley ?) Matthew Rhodon. Witnes my hand and - this 27th of Novem: 1652 The marke of Thomas Keene . Witnes Henry Rainer John Knight   20 Janu 1652 (1652/3) This will was proved by the oathes of Henry Rainer and John Knight and Execucion thereof Comitted to Mary Keene widdow and Principall Legatee and is Recorded ".

Record Book #14. page 16.

Mr Boulton   Will of Mr ffrancis Boulton. "I give unto my sone
his will   a Lawe Thomas Bassett all my estate either in debts
                  or otherwise that is in Virginia I give unto the
said Thomas Bassett and his sisters Susan (page torn away here) - Catren Sarah and to my Brother Hugh his child all my estate that is due to me in England either debts or Legasye to be equally divided between them A suite of Clothes that Mr Conyers promised to give me I give to Thomas Bassett   Witnes Michael Brooke   John Cousens marke John Paine his marke   20 June 1652 This will was proved in Court by the oathes of Michael Brooke and John Paine and execucon thereof was Comitted to Thomas Bassett Principall Legatee and is Recorded".

Note: One must respect the high regard in which this man held his stepson. B.F.

Mr Trussell his   John Trussell of Northumberland Co., sells to Jas.
Sale of Land to   Claughton 496 acres, originally patented by him,
James Claughton   Trussell, bordering on Kings Creek, etc. Dated 20th
                   January 1652 (1652/3). Signed John Trussell.
                   Witnesses: John Smith, Edmund Cingcleate his mark.
                   Recorded 20th January 1652 (1652/3).

Caption torn away. "I John Rosier doe by these presents acquitt release and discharge Robert Wyard his heirs or Assignes of and from all Dues Debts and Demands whatsoever from the beginning of the world to this present day being the 7th day of Novem: 1649 Jo Rosier   20 Janu 1652 This Discharge was Recorded ".

Record Book #14. page 17.

Mr Edw Tempest	"March the 29th 1652"
his Inventory	"A true and just Appraisment of the estate of Mr Edward Tempest deceased by us whose names are under-

written Mr John Hollowes Mr Walter Brodhurst Comr's: Mr John Rosier Clerke Mr Hugh Lee Appraisers" The following items are included:

Imp'rs 5 men servants one sicke boy at	5500 Tobacco
One great old chest	0050
4 little silver spoones 1 small trencher salt	0150
2 pewter candlesticks	0020
4 pare of damnified sheepskins gloves	0008
3 quire of paper	0003
5 doz of mildued damnified gloves	0060
one 3 gallon runlet of wyne	0030
1 quarter Caske of Drams halfe out	0100
4 Cases of Drams	0220
2 small gold ringgs	0130
Total	10826 Tobacco.

Recorded 20th Janu 1652 (1652/3)

John Dennis Junr	"An Inventory of the Goods of John Dennis Junr who
his Inventory	dyed at Wicocomocoe at John Dennis Senr the ultimo

July 1652 praised by Rich Budd Jo: Gresham and Jo Gamblin sworne before George ffletcher the 4th Septem 1652"

A bed and pillows two trading cloth blanketts and a white blankett praised at Tobco	250
A stuffe Cloke two stuffe sheets	080
4 yards of red Bayes	090
3 Coates and a pare of breeches of Island cloth	100
2 pare of gray stockings a hatt 2 capps a pare knitt gloves a cloth shute old	040
a Kamacooe old	020
a pare of bootes with a pare of spurrs and two pare new shooes	70
2 pare of drawers 3 shirts 5 plain bands a neckscloth 3 hankerchies 2 towells a looking glass	130
10 lb of Barbadus Indicoe	-
an old sea Chest and other things	020
a Bible and 7 other bookes	050
a silver Dram-cup and 3 s in money	-
a powter Aqua vitea bottle and dram cupp of the same	-
an Inckhorne	003

	915

Septem 4th 1652

Debts due to John Dennis Junr who dyed in Virginia at Jo'n Dennis Senr's house in Wicocomocoe the last day of July 1652

John Dennis Senr upon Accot	1026
Thomas Kingwell by bill	0148
Henry Hurst	0100
Daniel the Smith	0028

	1302

20 January 1652 This Inventory was Recorded The Marke of Richard Budd John Gresham The Marke of John Gamblin .
(see next page)

Record Book #14.   page 18.

John Dennis Senr his Accot of Jo: Dennis Junr his estate	"The Accompt of John Dennis Senr Administ'r of all and singular the goods and Chattels of John Dennis Junr decd late whilest he lived of Great Wicocomocoe in the County of Northumberland and Colony of Virginia	
	Imprs this Accomptant & Administrator doth charge himselfe with all the estate of the said decd contained in an inventory amounting unto the sume of	2217

Paid and laid out of the dec'd estate as followeth

Imprs this Accomptant and Administrator hath paid himselfe a debt due and oweing unto him by the dec'd in his life time for transporting the dec'ds goods from Newports-newes	400
Itm due from the decd to this Accomptante for nine months dyett	900
Itm for a funeralle Dinner	500
Itm for the decds washing and soap in his life time	100
Itm for travails and dyet at the Ordinary about getting the Ad'con	100
Itm to the Clerke of the Court for his fees	(sheet torn)

	2142

Soe it appeareth by this Accot that this Accomptant and Administrator hath got remaneing on his hands of the estate of the decd the sume of 0069

20 Janu 1652 (1652/3) This Acco was Recorded at the peticon of Barbary Dennis widd of the Ad'tor and Accomptant "

Note: The settlement of this estate interests me in showing about what an average man, of a certain position, would have at that time and place. It is what I would have had for instance. In fact uncomfortably close to my existing assets are the 2 pare of drawers, 8 books, a silver Dram cupp and 3 shillings in money.

Mr. and Mrs. Dennis, Senior, did the best they could to console themselves. The funeral dinner equalled five months board. Young John's uncanny habits of cleanliness were worthy of a Court entry. The accounting leaves nothing to be desired. We trust that the business trip to the Ordinary, expense detail omitted, did not hasten dear father's end.

Please note the exact meaning shown of the name of the city of Newport News.   Bev. Fleet.

- - Claughton his pattent	Patent from Sir William Berkeley to James Claughton for 250 acres in Northumberland Co. on a creek called Claughtons Creek, also adj. land of Mr Geo.
Higgins, etc. This land due for the transportation of 5 persons into the Colony. Their names not shown on record. Dated 20th Decem: 1650.	
James Claughton his Assigne'mt to Mr Rogers	Claughton assigns his right in the above to Mr John Rogers. Dated 20 Jan. 1652 (1652/3) Signed James Claughton, Wit: Tho Wilsford. Recorded 20th Jan. 1652 (1652/3)

Record Book #14. page 18.

Note: While the following entry may be long and dull, it is given in full for reasons that will be evident to anyone who has the time and patience to read it.   B.F.

Tho Sheppard and   "To all whom these presents shall come I Richard
James Claughton   Bennett Esqr Govern'r and Captaine Generall of
- - pattent   Virginia send greeting in our Lord God everlasting
Whereas by the Articles Dated at James Citty the 12th day of March 1651 concluded and signed by the Comiss'rs appointed by the Authority of Parl't for the reducing and settling and governing of Virginia it was provided that the previledge of ffifty Acres of Land for every person transported into this Colony should stand and be continued as formerly granted and whereas at a Grand Assembly Dated the 26th of Aprill 1652 it was provided that all Pattents should hereafter be signed under the Gov'nrs hand and the Secretaries and shal be accompted authentick and valid in law untill a Colony seale shal be appointed and provided   Now know yee that I the said Richard Bennett Esqr doe in the names of the Keepers of England - (line drawn through the noun England in the original) the Liberty of England by Authority of Parl't with the consent of the Councell of State give and grant unto Tho Sheppard and James Claughton three hundred acres of land lying and being in the County of Northumberland all - - (page torn away here) and South East upon the land of the plantacon of Mr Wil- Presly South East up upon the head of a Creek issueing out of Youocomocoe River Southwest and northwest upon the main woods The said land being due unto the said Thomas Sheppard and James Claughton by and for the transportation of six persons into the Colony all whose names are in records menconed under this Pattent To have and to hold the said land with his due share of all mines and mineralls therein contained with all rights and previledge of hunting hawkeing fishing and fowling with all woods and waters and rivers with all profitts Comodi'ties and hereditam'ts whatsoever in any wise belonging to the said land to them the said Thomas Sheppard and James Claughton their heirs and assignes forever in as large and ample man'er to all intents and purposes as is expressed in a Ch're (Charter) of Orders from the late Treasurer and Company Dated the 18th of Novem 1618 or by consequence may be justly collected out of the same or out of the L'res pattents whereon they are grounded yeilding and paying unto the Rent gatherers appointed thereunto for every fifty Acres of Land herein by these presents given and granted yearly at the feast of St Michael thearkangell (sic) the fee rent of one shilling wch paym't is to be made seaven yeares after the first grant or seating there of and not before Provided that if the said Thomas Sheppard or James Claughton their heirs or Assignes doe not plant or seat or cause to be planted or seated upon the said land within three yeares next ensueing that then it may and shal be lawfull for any adventuror or planter to make choise or seat thereupon   Given at James Citty und'r our hands this sixth day of May 1652: Ri Bennett   Wm Claiborne Secr ".

Record Book #14. page 19.

James Claughton his   Claughton assigns his interest in the above to
Assignment to   Sheppard. Dated - Jan. 1652 (1652/3)
Tho Sheppard   Signed James Claughton   Witnesses: John Trussell,
                       Rich fflynt.   Recorded 21 Jan. 1652 (1652/3).

Record Book #14. page 19.

Rich Hawkins his pattent	Patent. Sir Wm. Berkeley, etc., to Richard Hawkins, 100 acres in Northumberland Co., on the W. side of Nominye on S. side of Potowmacke river, adj. land of Thomas Waggell (or Weggett) and land of Thomas Rumsey, for transpt. of 2 persons into colony, their names not shown. Dated 30 Jan. 1650.
Richard Hawkins assignment to Edward Thompson	One half of above assigned by Hawkins to Thompson. Dated 11 ffeb 1651 (1651/2). Signed The Marke of Rich: Hawkins. The marke of Tho Waggett (sic).
Edw Thompson and Rich Hawkins their Assignment to Mr Speke	Thompson and Hawkins assign above to Mr Tho Speke, gent. Dated 18th Jan. 1652 (1652/3) Signed Edward Thompson Richard Hawkins his marke The marke of Henry Brooke Wm Hardich. Acknowledged by Wm Hardich, attorney for Thompson and Hawkins. Recorded 20th Jan. 1652. (1652/3).
Edw Thomson and Rich Hawkins their l're of att	Power of Atty, Thompson and Hawkins to "our loving friend William Hardich". Dated 18th Jan 1652. Signed Edw: Thomson The marke of Richard Hawkins. Witnesses: Hen Brookes, Tho Youll.
Ralph Elstons lre of Att to Wm Hardich	Power of Atty. Ralph Elston in the Co. of Northumberland, planter, to Wm. Hardich. Dated 19th Jan. 1652 (1652/3). Signed Ralph Elston. Witnesses: Edward Thomson, Gaphaniel Smith (sic).

Record Book #14. page 20.

Jone Gamblin her Depo	"Jone Gamblin aged about 23 yeares sweareth That Cyprian Bishop came into the house of - (page torn away here) fflynt and asked the said fflynt If he kept a Bawdy-house and he answered no if you doe it it is no more than your mother did before you by report And further sweareth not Decem: the 29th 1652 Geo ffletcher 20 Janu Recorded this Depo".
Sarah Bishopp her depo	"The Deposition of Sarah Bishop taken the 17th of Janu 1652 Sweareth that Sarah Bowyer in other discourse told the said Sarah Bishop That Dorothy fflynts mother kept a Baudy house in England to wch the said Sarah Bishop made Answeare that that could not be for she knew her mother then the said Sarah Bowyer made Answere that Thomas Prichett tolde her soe and further saith not The marke of Sarah Bishopp Jurat Coram me Geo ffletcher".

Record Book #14. page 20.

Cyprian Bishop his Depo	"Cyprian Bishop deposeth the same with this Depont (signed) Cyprian Bishop his marke 20 Janu Recorded these Depo".

"Jan the 15th 1652" (1652/3)

Tho Hopkins
his Depo

"Thomas Hopkins aged 34 years or thereabouts sworne and examined saith That being in discourse with Richard fflynt he the said fflynt tolde this Depont that Cyprian Bishop came into the house of the said fflynt and asked him if he kept a Baudy house who replyed no why doe you aske such a question the said Bishop Answeared that Bowyers wife reported his wife lay in a young mans armes in the house of the said fflynt and that he the said Bishop would have Bowyers wife whipt The said fflynt replyed that that would not have her whipt The said Bishop Answeared againe that if that would (page torn away here) - - her whipt he knew what would the said fflynt - - (page torn away) (asked) what that was Bishop replyed that Bowyers wife said the said fflynts wifes mother kept a Bawdy house in England and further the said ffl nt told this Depont that he tooke it not as a neighborly ourtesy from (page torn) said Bishop because he told the said fflynt of it - -(page torn) - the said Bishop and his wife had a falling out with - Bowyer's wife and further saith not   Thomas Hopk-   Jurat Coram me Geo ffletcher".

Rich fflynt
his Depo

"Rich fflynt saith That Cyprian Bishop told this Depont all what Tho Hopkins deposeth and further saith that the said Bishop bid Wm Raughton speake to Mr Bowyer to make haste home and see his wife whipt before he went 20 Janu 1652 Jurat - (page torn)- - - Mottrom ".

Caption torn
away

Power of Atty. Gabriel Odyer to "my beloved friend William Thomas" regarding a suit botw. Odyer and John Cunery (?). Dated 16 Jan 1652 (1652/3). Signed Gabriel Odyer. Witness Walter Brodhurst. Recorded 20th Janu 1652 (1652/3).

Wm Reynolds
his Depo

"Wm Reynolds aged 50 yeares or thereabouts being sworne and examined saith that this Depont was desired by Mrs Hawkins the wife of Thomas Hawkins to goe with her and Mr Broughton to be witnes of a Bill of sale of a Cow wch she said her husband had bought of Richard White and when they came thither the Cowe was not at home But he refused to make a Bill of sale of the Cowe till he had spoken with and come to Acco with the said Hawkins The said White said The Calfe was in the penn and the Cow would come to her Calfe ere long and then he would deliver the Cowe to John Squibb And further saith not Wm Reynolds his marke 20 Janu 1652 Jurat in Cur " (1652/3)

Note: It would seem that the character of the virtuous Cyprian would leave something to be desired.   B.F.

97

Record Book #14.   page 20.

Wm Reynolds   "Wm Reynolds aged 50 yeares or thereabouts being
his Depo   sworne and examined saith That he heard Elias
                   Richardson say that he was ashamed to looke Mr
Higgins in the face because he had not brought up Mr Higgins his Bills
He said he was paid in a way somehow and came there but it did him
little good and further this Depont saith not   Wm Reynolds his marke
20 Janu: 1652 Jurat in Cur "   (1652/3).

Rich Clare   "Richard Clare aged 30 yeares or thereabouts being
his Depo   sworne and examined saith That he heard Elias Rich-
                   ardson say that he was ashamed to go to Mr Higgins
his house because he had not brought up his writeings but what writeings this Depont knoweth not and further this Depont saith not   Richard
Clare his marke   20 Janu 1652 Jurat in Cur". (1652/3)

Note: These two Depositions, exhibiting the unbusinesslike methods of
Elias Richardson are a relief after the Bishop-Flint episode. All is not
well with my conscience for including transcripts of that. Were these
people ancestors of mine I'd not be grateful to anyone who broadcast
over the country such genealogical detail.   Beverley Fleet.

Tho Blagg   Thomas Blagg of Northumberland County files his
his marke   mark for cattle. Recorded 20 Jan. 1652. (1652/3).

Mr Pope   Mr. Nathaniel Pope of Northumberland County records
his marke   his mark for cattle. 20 Jan. 1652. (1652/3).

Record Book #14.   page 21.

Jo Waddy   "John Waddy aged 33 years or thereabouts being
his Depo   sworne and examined saith" that Mr. Nicholas
                   Morris did preffer John Gresham two hundred pounds
                   of Tobacco at John Essex's, in part payment which
                   Thomas Coggan should pay to Gresham, for the cow
                   that was in suit.
                   Signed   John Waddy his marke.
                   "20 Janu 1652 Jurat in Curia" (1652/3)

Record Book #14. page 21.

"Levies for Northumberland County"

To be added to this yeares Levies of the Arreares of the last	2531
To Mr Trussell for Burgesses charges 1651 & killing a wolf	1500
for Mr Presly Tho Wilsford & Mr Lees charges of Burgeship 1651	3990
for Mr Speke & Mr Baldridge their charges of Burgeship 1651	3490
for Colo Mottrom & Leift Colo ffletcher their charge of Burgeship 1652	5400
for 8 wolves	0800
to Goodman Pare 2 lb the poll	0780
to Mr Smith for carrying a felon to the Sherr of Lancaster and two men with him	0180
to the Clerke of the Assembly	0300
for powd'r and shott @ 6 lb Tob per poll	2340
for Contry Levies from James Towne at 22 lb Tob'co per poll	8580
for sallary at 10 lb Tobco per Cent for Collecting	2989

	32880

390 persons is 85 lb Tobco per poll

20 Janu: 1652 This Levie was made up by th- (page torn) - of Northumberland "

Record Book #14. page 21.

Tho Philpott   Thomas Philpott of Wiccocomocoe in Northumberland
his marke   records mark for cattle 20th Jan.1652. (1652/3).

Note: Let us assume that the origin of this honorable old Kentish name is after the manner of the slogan used in the time of President Cleveland, ie. the 'full dinner pail'. Nevertheless I would change it if it were mine.   B. F.

Mr Knights acquit   "R'd the 20 June 1652 of George Knott in part of a
to Geo Nott   greater sum the sume of 4549 lb Tobo By me Peter
                    Knight". Recorded 20th Jan. 1652 (1652/3).

Beckets rect of   "Rd for the a/c of Mr John Manning one hhd of
Wm Allenson   Tobco of Wm Allenson the 14th of January weighing
                    436 pound grosse by me   John Beckett ".
                    Recorded 20th January 1652. (1652/3).

Record Book #14. page 21.

Caption Mutilated	Bill binding Edward Hudson to pay to John Dandy 670 lb. tobo. on or before 15th Oct. next. Dated 27th Sept 1651. Signed Edward Hudson his marke. Witnesses: WM Cocke, Hugh Lee.
- Danby his Assignment of Edw Hudsons Bill to Mr Smith & Wilsford	John Danby assigns Hudson's bill to Mr. Sam Smith and Mr. Tho. Wilsford. No date shown. Signed John Danby his marke. Witnesses Jo: Davies, Rich Atherton (?) his mark.
Richard Ingle his lre of Attr to Capt Cornwaleys	Power of Atty. Richard Ingle of Wapping in the County of Middlesex Marryner to Thomas Cornewallis gent. to collect debts listed below. Dated 8th Sept 1647 "and in the three and twentieth yeare of the Reigne of our Souverign Lord King Charles". Signed Richard Ingle.

Witnesses: Wm Eltonhed
          ffra Manestry No'tius Publicus
          John Browne his servt.

Note: The hand of Death, swiftly and dreadfully passed through that little piece of paper. Churches of England and Rome.   B.F.

Record Book #14. page 22.

25th of Novem   "Inventory of the Papers receaved of Capt Ingle for
   1646   Goods and Debts in Virginia and Mary-Land"

1 A receite of Nathaniel Popes bearing Date the 24th of March 1644 for
     certaine goods marked E & R *6* with some other things left with
     him by Capt Ingle

2 A Bill from Mr Tho Gerrard for 4 lb C 1/2 of Beaver & 864 lb of Tobeo
     bearing date 15th ffebruary 1643   (1643/4)

3 A note of Barnaby Jacksons for half his stocke of Hoggs bearing Date
     the 14th of March 1644   (1644/5)

4 Thomas Baldridge his Bill bearing date the 5 of Aprill for 500
     weight of Tobco & Caske

5 & 6 A Bill & noate of John Sturmans the one dated the 10th of Aprill
       1645 for satisfaction of Tenn pound of powder The other Dated
       the 4th Aprill 1645 for 900 weight of Tobco & caske

7 A Copy of a Judgem't against Thomas Bradnax for 900 weight of Tobco
     & Caske Dated the 18th of March 1642   (1642/3)

8 An acknowledgement of Capt William Stone dated the 10th of Aprill
     1645 for the receipt of a Bill of Argoll Y- (page torn away but
     this name is Argoll Yeardley) Esq for 9860 weight of Tobco &
     Caske And another Mr Wm Andrews for 14 hhds of Tobco

(continued next page)

Record Book #14. page 22.

Inventory of the Papers Received of Capt. Ingle, etc.,(continued)

9 A Bill of Capt Wm Ropers dated the third of Aprill 1644 for 300 weight of Rowle Tobco

10 John Hinmans bill dated the 8th of ffeb: 1644 for 142 lb Tobco in caske

11 A Bill from John Hallowes & John Warell (or Wavell) Dated the 24 of March 1644 (1644/5) for 700 weight of Tobco & Caske

12 Doct'r Waldrons noate for 20 s. dated the 13th of Aprill - - page torn away.

13 An Accompt of Mrs Wheatleys of Ackomacke for 3000 lb of Tobco with an Invoice of goods   A Bill of Mr Wm Branth- - (page torn) dated the 10th of ffebruary 1640 (1640/1) for 1400 weight of Tobco & Caske.

14 & 15 A receipt of Capt Stones for Goods receaved of Mrs Wheatleys as also another of Capt Stones for other goods receaved of Capt Ingle

16 A receipt of Capt Wm Ropers for divers accompts due at Ackomacke amounting to the quanity of 4563 lb of Tobco & Caske wch is since in the hands of Capt Wm Stone

"This Inventory or Schedule with tho lre of Atturney was Recorded the 10th of ffebruary 1652 Juxta cr"

Ralph Horsly his acquittance to Tho Wilsford	"18th ffeb 1652" "R'd the day & yeare above written of Tho Wilsford" 960 lb. tobo. in full for an Order of Court 25th November last. Signed The Marke of Ralph Horsly. Witness, Hugh Lee. Recorded 18th Feb. 1652 (1652/3)
Wm Warder his pattent	Grant from Sir Wm. Berkeley to William Warder 550 acres due for transportation of 11 persons, names not shown, into the colony. Dated 19 Oct. 1643. Signed William Berkeley. Recorded 26th Feb. 1652. (1652/3)
John Rogers his marke	John Rogers of Northumberland County records his mark for cattle 26th Feb. 1652 . (1652/3).

Record Book #14. page 23.

Tho Knight his sale to Mr Rosier	Jan 30 1652. (1652/3). Knight sells to John Rosier cattle and 2 guns. Signed Thomas Knight his marke. John Powell, Thomas Philpott. Recorded 10th Mar. 1652. (1652/3).
John Cooke his will	The will of John Cooke "living upon Appamattacke". To Becca Ryall a cow and a calf. Rest of estate to "my welbeloved friend Mr Nathaniel Pope". Dated 6th August 1652. Signed The marke of John Cooke. Witnesses Richard Nicoll, Abraham Jerman. Proved 10th March 1652. (1652/3).
John Chambers his pattent	Grant. Richard Bennett Esq., etc., 150 acres for transpt. of 3 persons into the colony. Dated 10th October 1652. Signed Ri Bennett, W Claiborne, Secy.
Caption mutilated.	George Colclough, Attorney of John Chambers, assigns interest in foregoing patent to Phillip Carpenter. Dated 20 Mar. 1652 (1652/3). signed Geo. Colclough. Witness, Tho Wilsford.
- - Chambers his lre of Attur to Mr Colclough	Power of Atty. John Chambers to Geo. Colclough to transfer above land to Carpenter. Dated 9th March 1652 (1652/3). signed John Chambers. Witness, Samuel Smith. Recorded 10 Mar. 1652/3.
Phillip Carpenter his assignment of a Pattent to Edward Henley The Pattent is Recorded in the 75 leafe of the old book of Records	Carpenter assigns his right in a patent to Edward Henley. Dated 20 Oct. 1652. Signed Phillip Carpenter. Witnesses: Hugh Lee, Peircy Hamond his marke. 10th March 1652/3 this assignment was ack. in Court by Carpenter and the patent Recorded 10th June 1653.

Note: The above caption refers to 'the old book of Records'. Therefore there was at one time a book pre-dating #2 and #14. Of course there is #1, that being but a few scattered sheets, thought to be the remains of an old Court Order Book.   B.F.

Mr Hallowes Assignmt of a Pattent (of 500 acres of Land assigned him from Jo'n Walton) to Jo'n Jenkins	John Hallowes assigns right in patent to John Jenkins. Dated 10th March 1652/3. Signed Jo: Hallowes. Witness, Th Wilsford. This assignment ack. in Court by Hallowes 10th March 1652/3. The original gives the date of Recording as 20th September 1652.

Record Book #14. page 23.

John Dennis Senr his Inventory	"An Inventory of the estate of John Dennis decd., taken and appraised by us whose names are here underwritten and sworne before Mr Geo ffletcher this 28th of January Ano D'm 1652". (1652/3) Total 15850 lb. Tobo. Signed: Richard Budd, Richard fflynt, Cyprian Bishop. Recorded 10th March 1652/3.

Record Book #14. page 24.

Rich Ball his marke	Richard Ball of Youocomocoe in Northumberland Co. records mark for cattle and hogs. 17 March 1652/3.
Richard Turney - - -	Richard Turney of Northumberland Co., sells Hugh Lee a cow. Dated 15 April 1653. Signed Richard Turney. Witnesses: ffrancis Clay, William Bacon. Recorded 20 April 1653.

Tho Hailes "Thomas Hailes aged 44 yeares or thereabouts being
his Depo   sworne and examined saith That this Depont when he
            lived with Mr Trussell heard Elias Richardson say
that he was ashamed to goe in to Mr Higgins because he had not
brought up his Bills wch he said were paid but he said the next time
he came he would bring them or else he would never see his face more
and further this Depont saith not Tho Hailes his mark 10 March 1652
Jurat in Cur ". (1652/3).

Tho Bailes "Thomas Bailes aged 26 yeares or thereabouts being
his Depo   sworne and examined saith That since John Gresham
            recovered a cow with her increase of Tho Coggin
wch were in the possession of Mr Nicho: Morris" etc. signed Tho
Bailes his marke. 10th March 1652 Jurat in Cur. (1652/3).

- - Agreem't   An agreement that there be a division of hogs and
betweene Simon crop jointly owned by Richardson and Allam before
Richardson and Richardson was married. "Also wee are both agreed
Jeremy Allam   to pay all the debts and ingagemts that wee stand
                ingaged for excepting what debts the sd Richardson
made about his marriage". Dated 15 May 1653.
Witnesses: Mich Brooke   Signed   Simon Richardson
           Wm Wildey   Jeremy Allam
Recorded 20th May 1653.

Record Book #14. page 25.

Wm Allenson his pattent	Patent from Sir Wm Berkeley to William Allenson, Senr., 150 acres, adj. land of George Crouch, for transportation of 3 persons. Dated 21 December 1650.

Record Book #14. page 25.

Wm Allenson his assignment of a Pattent to Walter Weekes	Allenson assigns right in foregoing patent to Weekes. Dated 12th April 1653. Signed Wm Allenson his marke. Witness, Henry Toppin his mark.

Wm Thomas his sale of Land to Hulst & Woodes	Wm Thomas sells 200 acres for 1000 lb tobo., to John Hulst and Charles Woodes. They to choose land from 400 acres, all 200 acres on either one side or the other of the Great Wicocomoco river. Dated Dec.

10th 1652. Signed Wm Thomas. Witnesses Tho Kedbye, The mark of Anthony Linton. Ack. and Recorded 20 May 1653.

Caption destroyed.	Patent. Sir Wm Berkeley to Jeffery Gooch, gent., 500 acres in Northumberland Co., on S. side of Great Wicocomoco River, for transp. of 10 persons into the colony. Dated 30 January 1650/1.

" At a Court holden at James Citty the 31st of January 1641 Sr ffrancis Wyatt Knt Govn'r etc Capt Wm Peirce Mr Geo Mineffe Mr Argol Yeardley Mr Rich Bennett Esqrs

The ord'r of James Towne Court for land for Mr Gooche	Upon a surrend'r of a Pattent for 500 acres at the ffalls granted to Mr Jeffery Gooche weh canot in regard of the remateness from the English plantations be securely seated without great charges The Court

hath therefore Ordered that he shall have leave to take up soe much Land in an other place in right of the said Pattent Extr & examtr per me John Meade This is a true Copy of the Ord'r per me Abraham Moone
20 May 1653 This pattent and Ord'r of James Towne Court were Recorded " .

Note: Well Mr. Jeffery Gooch had much better kept his 500 acres on the site of future Richmond, and stood the great charges, rather than have taken what he got in Northumberland Co. B.F.

Mr Turney his pattent	Patent. Sir William Berkeley etc., to Richard Turney, 2109 acres in Northumberland Co., abutting S. on Potomack River, E. upon a great marsh,

W. upon a Bay and N. upon a Creek issuing out of the said bay. This land commonly called Doggs Island. This land due for the transportation of 42 persons into the colony. Dated 8th July 1651.

- - Turney his - of land to - Phillips	20th May 1653. Richard Turney sells land in the above patent to David Phillips. Signed Richard Turney. Witness, Th Wilsford. Ack. and Recorded 20th May 1653.

Record Book #14, page 26.

Mr Lake his Assurance of Land to Mr Colclough	Richard Lake, gent., formerly sold to George Colclough certain land "called Hulls Thickett being the moyety of - land formerly belonging to Mr Thomas Broughton and the said Lake". Dated 8th Jan. 1652/3. Signed Rich Lake. Witnesses John Mottrom, Simon Richardson.

Mr Lakes lre of Attur to Tho Kedby	Power of Atty. Rich: Lake to Thomas Kedby to make above sale. Dated 8th Jan. 1652. Signed "I shall be your thankfull friend Rich Lake. Ack. and Recorded 20th May 1653.

Abraham Janssons lre of Attur to John Johnson Bosteware	Power of Atty, Abraham Jansson of Grast in Holland to "my trusty friend skipper John Johnson Bosteware to receive from Capt Vane in Kent of John Hodge in Mary Land and of Mr Stranger in Accamacke all of them living in Virginia all and singular such debts" as they owe. Dated in Amsterdam 7 Sept 1651. Signed Abraham Jansson. Witnesses John Bee, Henry B-ne, Joseph Steyne.

- - Janssen his - - Attur to - - Michael	Power of Atty. John Jansson "unto my loveing friend John Michael" to transact business in Virginia. Signed thus: "Witnes of my hand and seale Ano 1652 this 29th of July aborde the shipp ffarewell in Virginia reddy to set sale from Accamacke John Janssen". Witnesses: Wm Whittington, Cornelius Cornelison. Recorded 20th May 1653.

Jacob Derickson his lre of Attur to John Johnson Bosteware	Power of Attorney "Skipper Jacob Derickson late master of the Honny barrel" to "my trusty friend John Johnson Bosteware" to collect debts from John Hodge of Mary-Land and John Haynie of Chickacone. Dated 7th Sept. 1651. Signed Jacob Derickson. Witnesses: John Ber, Joseph Steynes. Recorded 20th May 1653.

John Jansson his lre of Attur to John Michael	Power of Atty. from Skipper Jacob Derickson to Jansson, assigned over to "my Loveing Nephew John Michael". Dated 29th July 1652. Signed John Jansson. Witnesses: Wm Whittington, Cornelius Cornelison. Recorded 20 May 1653.

John Michael his lre of Attur to Wm Thomas	Power of Atty. John Michael of Northampton County in Virginia to "my trusty friend Mr Wm Thomas" to collect debts in Northumberland Co. Dated 18th May 1653. Signed John Michael. Witnesses: The Marke of Edward Coles, Joseph Harrison.

Record Book #14. page 27.

Giles Taverner his lre of Attur to Rich Holden	Power of Atty. from Tavernor to Holden to collect a debt from Hercules Bridges. Dated 27th Dec.1652 Recorded 20th May 1653.

Note: The day of reconing has come. B.F.

Capt Hackett his lre of Attur to Wm Thomas	Power of Atty., Hackett to "my loving friend Wm Thomas, to collect debts. Dated 15 ffeb 1652.(52/3) Signed Thomas Hackett. Witness, Peter Knight. Recorded 20 May 1653.
Tho Saffall his lre of Attur to Wm Thomas	Power of Atty. Saffell to Thomas to collect from Robert Butt. Dated 15 Jan. 1652/3. Signed Tho Saffall his mark, Witness, John Gatehouse. Recorded 20 May 1653.
Caption destroyed	Mr Augustine Hull of Nomine in the County of Northumberland records mark for cattle and hogs 20 May 1653.
Ann Reynolds her Depo	"Ann Reynolds aged 37 yeares or thereabouts sworne and examined saith That Elias Richardson came to this Deponts house and said he was going to Mr Trussells but said also that he was ashamed to goe thither because he had not brought up Mr Higgins his Bills x x ". Signed Ann Reynolds her marke. "20 May 1653 Jurat in Cur".
John Lee his Deposition	"The Deposition of John Lee aged 36 yeares or thereabouts sworne and examined saith That to his knowledge he heard Mr Abbott say that he had rec'd of Capt Brent all the Tobco that Capt Brent owed the said Abbott x x x And further saith not Recognitum Coram me W Claiborne Sec 13 May 1653 20 May 1653 This Depos was Recorded".

Record Book #14. page 28.

Tho Gaskins his Depo	"The Deposition of Thomas Gaskins aged 52 yeares or thereabouts sworne and examined and saith That John Hulet and Wm Thomas being at Thomas Gaskins his house and fell out at words and the said Wm Thomas called John Hulet Rogue and comon Rogue and said that he would prove him a Rogue and if he did he would have him marked for a Rogue in the shoulder before he came from Court and that he fledd out of Virginia about the deth of his wife or else he might have been hanged and that he was accounted a Towne-Bull And further saith not Tho Gaskin Nicholas Morris 20 May 1653 This Depo was Recorded".

Note: This time we believe Mr. Thomas, but still remain a little suspicious of Mr. Morris.   B.F.

Record Book #14. page 27.

Isaac Weaver   "Isaac Weaver aged 40 yeares or thereabouts being
his Depo   sworne and examined saith That at the house of Tho
Gaskins he this Depont heard Wm Thomas call John
Hulett Rogue and said he would prove him a Rogue and that he was taxed
in Virginia for Murther and further said that the said Hulet was a
Com'on Towne Bull And further saith not Isaac Weaver his marke 20
May 1653 Jurat in Cur ".

- -   "Jno Catanceau aged 17th yeares or thereabouts
               being sworne and examined saith That this Depont
brought up a Bill in wch Angell Harwood stands bound to Elias Richardson for the paymt of ffourteene or sixteene pounds sterling And the
said Bill was lost by this Depont and further saith not John
Catanceau 20 May 1653 Jurat in Cur"

Record Book #14. page 28-badly mutilated.

Alice Stanley Mutilated. "Alice Stanley aged 19 or thereabouts
her Depo   sworn and examined saith That Henry Barnes tooke
               John H- - - to Thomas Orley out of the Cropp and
intended to carry him - - - the Country and forced him to goe along
with - - - - meanes the said Orlye lost his Cropp and further saith not
Alice Stanley her marke 20 May 1653 Jurat in Cur".

John Hill his   "John Hill aged 26 years or thereabouts being
Deposition   sworne and examined saith That Henry Barnes came
                with a Cocked Pistoll and swore he would kill him
if he would not goe with him and thereupon forced this Depont to goe
with - - to the great losse and damage of his said master and further
saith not John Hill 20 May 1653 Jurat in Cur "

Mr Turney   "Richard Turney aged 44 yeares or thereabouts being
his Depo   sworne and examined saith That this Depont paid for
               the use of Mr Sampson Calvert Clerk Two hundred
pounds of Tobco and Caske to the Ordinary of Mary-Land and never rec'd
any satisfaction for the same wch 200 lb Tobco and Caske this Depont
hath Assigned to John Danby with a Bill of Eight hundred pounds of
Tobco and Caske and further saith not Richard Turney 20 May 1653
Jurat in Cur".

John Swanson   John Swanson of Great Wicocomocoe in the County of
his marke   Northumberland records mark for cattle and hogs
               10th June 1653.

Richard Dennis Richard Dennis of Great Wicocomoco in the County of
his marke   Northumberland records mark for cattle and hogs
               10th June 1653.

Natha Hellen   Natha Hellen of Great Wicocomocoe in the County of
his mark   Northumberland records mark for cattle and hogs
               10th June 1653.

Record Book #14. page 28.

Pascoe Dennis his marke	Pascoe Dennis of Wicocomocoe in the County of Northumberland records mark for cattle and hogs 10th June 1653.
Caption torn away	John Trussell sells a heifer to Matthew Rhoden. Dated 18th May 1653. Signed John Trussell. Witnesses: James Claughton, Edmond Sincler his mark.
Matthew Rhoden his gift of a heifer to Eliza Trussell	"Know all men that I Matthew Rhoden doe freely give to Elizabeth Trussell the daughter of Mr John Trussell and Mary his now wife this within named heifer x x ". Dated 20 May 1653. Signed Matthew Rhoden. Witnesses: Tho Kedby, Hugh Lee. Recorded 14th June 1653.
Tho Rice his acquitt to Corbet Pedle	Release from debts to date. Dated 2 Jan. 1652/3. Signed The mark of Thomas Rice, John Cotanceau. Recorded 20 July 1653.

"The oath of Surveyor Administered to Gervase Dodson"

Mr Dodsons oath   "You shall sweare well and truly to searve the
- Surveyor   Commonwealth of England und'r the Governem't of
                   this Collony as a Surveyor And according to the
best of your ability and conscience to measure and lay out Land rightly
justly truely and indifferently for those by whom you shall be imployed
in it or whom it shall concearne Soe help - - God etc Ger Dodson
Novem 28. 1652 Juratr W Claiborne Trer 21 July 1653 This oath was
Recorded"

Record Book #14. page 29.

Mr Dodson his pattent	Patent signed by Sir William Berkeley for 1600 acres due for transp. of 32 persons into the colony. Dated 1 Feb. 1660/1. Recorded 21 July 1653.

Mr Rosier and   "Know all men by these presents That wee John
Corbet Pedell   Hallowes the Atturney of Mr John Rosier and
their Assumpsit   Corbett Pedell doe seavr' ingage our selves in the
                  Assumpsit of 5000 pounds weight of Tobco & Caske
to stand to the Arbitracon D- - sentence and Decree of what persons
the abovesaid Mr Hallowes shall make choice on to end and determine a
Controversy betweene the said Mr Rosier and Corbet Pedell lately depending in Northumberland County C- and for the true preformance hereof wee the said John Hallowes and Corbet Pedell have interchangably
sett our hands the 30th of July 1653   Jo: Hallowes Corbet Pedle
Test Walter Brodhurst Jo: Tewe 1 August 1653 This Assumpsit was
Recorded".

Record Book #14. page 29.

Wm Hardich his acquitt to Jo Hiller	Hardich acquits Hiller from all debts. Dated 15th Feb. 1652/3. Signed Will Hardich. Witnesses: Walter Brodhurst, Peter fflippen his marke. Recorded 3 Aug. 1653.
Tho Boys his acquittance to John Hiller	Thomas Boys acquits Hiller from all debts. Dated 3rd Aug. 1653. Signed Thomas Boys his marke. Witnesses: John Pitt, Th Wilsford. Rec. 3 aug. 1653.
Caption torn.	John Kent of the County of Northumberland records his mark for cattle and hogs, 27th August 1653.

-h Holdens Bill
- Henry Vincent

"I Richard Holden Blacksmith living upon Youscomicoe necke upon Potomacke river in Virginia" stands indebted to "Henry Vincent planter in Yorke in Virginia" 3000 lb. tobo. payable 10 Nov. next. Gives as security his plantation, crops, cattle, "or whatsoever is mine". Dated 18 Aug. 1653. Signed The marke of Richard Holden. Witnesses: Thomas Young, the marke of Wm Walker. Recorded 19th Sept. 1653.

- - Cole makeing
- to John Armsby
- - owes for paymt
- - a Boy

Bill binding Richard Cole, Merchant, to deliver to John Armsbye of Nominye "by the last of December next at furthest or sooner if I please a youth servant sound in his body and limbs to the appearance of any honest men for performance of whereof I binde over unto the said Armsbye three cowes now goeing at Goodman Bennetts the Carpenter and the Ladd to serve seaven yeares at least". Dated 8th of April 1653. Signed Richard - (page torn). Witnesses: Tho Speke. John Tow-. Recorded 19 Sept 1653

Record Book #14. page 30.

Wm Vincent
his pattent

Grant. Sir Wm. Berkeley to Wm Vincent, 600 acres on the North side of a creek commonly called Dividing Creek, adj. land of James Willis and also the land of John Waddy. This 600 acres due for transp. of 12 persons into the colony, names not shown in the record. Dated 3rd April 16- (illegible)

Wm Vincent his
Assignment of a
Pattent to John
Ingram

Foregoing patent assigned by Vincent to Ingram. Dated 27th Sept. 1651. Signed William Vincent. Witnesses: Peter Knight, The marke of John Dennis. Recorded 20 September 1653.

An Agreemt betweene
Jo'n Ingram and
Wm Vincent

An agreement. Vincent assigning to Ingram 300 acres. being 1/2 of a patent lying on Divideing Creek in ffleets bay. Vincent to have the neck he is now seated upon and John Ingram to have Cockorowses (?) neck, the balance to be equally divided. Dated 16th July 1651. Signed Wm Vincent. Witnesses: W. Claiborne, David Spiller his marke. Recorded 20 Sept. 1653.

Record Book #14. page 30.

Caption torn.	Grant. Sir William Berkeley to John Ingram and Richard fflynt 406 acres upon Dividing Creek, adj. land of Wm Vincent and that of John Waddy. Of this land 250 acres was granted to David Pole on 10th December 1638 and by him assigned to John Ingram, the balance due for the transportation of persons, names not shown, into the colony. Dated 10 April 1651.
Richd fflynt his sale of Land to John Ingram	Flint sells above land to Ingram. Dated 20th Sept. 1653. Signed Ri fflynt. Witnesses: Richard Turney, Tho Wilsford. Recorded 20 Sept. 1653.
James Macgreggor and Hugh ffouch their pattent	Grant. Sir William Berkeley to Macgreggor and Fouch, 300 acres in Northumberland Co., lying on Potomac River, on Sandy point at Chebanks Creekemouth, for transp. of 6 persons, names not shown, into the colony. Dated 29th July 1650.

Record Book #14. page 31.

James Macgreggor & Hugh ffouch their Assignmt of their pattent to John Hull	Foregoing assigned to Hull. Dated 18th Sept. 1652. Signed "Hugh ffouch James Macgreggor their marks". Witnesses: John Haynie, Samuell Nicholls. Recorded 20 Sept. 1653.
James Macgreggor & Hugh ffouch their pattent for Land	Grant. By Richard Bennett, Esq., etc. to Macgreggor and Fouch 394 acres in Northumberland Co., adj. foregoing patent, for transp. of 8 persons into the colony. Dated 5th April 1653.
James Macgreggor & Hugh ffouch their assignmt of a pattent to John Hull	Foregoing patent assigned to John Hull. Dated 20th Sept. 1653. Signed The marke of Hugh ffouch The marke of James Macgreggor. Witnesses: "Witnes by me Tho Kedby", Tho Wilsford. Rec. 20 Sept. 1653.
Caption worn away.	Grant. Sir William Berkeley to Hugh ffouch and James Macgreggor 800 acres in Northumberland Co., adj. above land, for transp. of 16 persons into the colony. Dated 3rd April 1651.
James Macgreggor his assignmt of a pattent to Hugh ffouch	Macgreggor assigns his interest in foregoing patent to Fouch. Dated 20th Sept. 1653. Signed James Macgreggor his marke. Witnesses Ger Dodson, John Hull. Recorded 20th Sept. 1653.

Record Book #14. page 31.

George Nott his pattent	Grant. Sir William Berkeley to George Nott, senr., 200 acres in Northumberland "on the west side of the head of Youocomocoo River abutting South East upon the head of the said river Southwest upon an Indian Bridge and a Vallye Northwest and North east upon the maine woods". 50 acres being due to Nott by assignment of George Berry and the other 150 acres granted for the transportation of 3 persons into this colony. Dated 22nd December 1650.
George Nott his assignmt of a pattent to Mr Knight	Nott assigns above to Mr Peter Knight. Dated 30th January 1652/3. Signed Geo Nott his marke. Witnesses: Natha Hickman, Rich Holden. Recorded 20th Sept. 1653.

Record Book #14. page 32.

Edward Coles and Tho Kingwell their pattent	Grant. Sir Wm. Berkeley to Coles and Kingwell 494 acres adj. land of Capt. Wm Claiborne Esq., and upon Coles Creek. 300 acres due by assignment from John Gamblin and 194 acres due for transpt. of 4 persons into the colony. Dated 20 Dec. - (year torn away)
Tho Kingwell his sale of Land to Edw Coles	Kingwell sells his share in foregoing to Coles. Dated 9th Sept. 1653. Signed Tho Kingwell. Witnesses: Ri fflynt, Tho Sheapard his marke.
Edward Coles his sale of Land to Jo'n Michael	Coles sells above land to John Michael, excepting 80 acres to Henry Smith. Dated 20th Sept. 1653. Signed Edward Coles. Witnesses: Geo C- (page torn), Ri fflynt. Recorded - Sept 1653.
Caption torn away	Grant. Sir Wm. Berkeley to John Bennett 200 acres for transp. of 4 persons into the colony. Dated 29th - 1651.
John Bennett his Assignmt of - Pattent to - Broughton and Mr Ashton	Bennett assigns the above 200 acres to Thomas Broughton and Charles Ashton. Date torn away. Signed John Bennett. Witnesses: Wm Thomas, Hugh Lee. Recorded - Sept. 1653.
John Hull his pattent	Grant. Sir William Berkeley to John Hull 200 acres adj. land of John Earle for transp. of 4 persons. Dated 18th October 1650.
John Hull his sale of Land to Tho Hailes	Entry mutilated. Hull sells foregoing land to Tho Hailes. Dated - - 1652. Signed John Hull his marke. Witnesses: Hugh Lee, John Davies his marke. Recorded 20th September 1653.

Record Book #14. page 33.

Tho Sheapard his sale of Land to Lewes Gilman	Sheapard sells 150 acres to Gilman formerly granted to Tho Sheapard and James Claughton 6th May 1652. This deed dated 18th Sept. 1653. Signed Tho Sheaphard. Witnesses: Tho Philp (sic), Rich Holden his marke. Recorded 20th Sept. 1653.
Tho Sheapard his sale of Land to Mr fflynt This pattent is Recorded folio 18 of this Book	Sheapard sells Richard fflynt 1/2 of 150 acres. Dated - Sept'165-. Signed The Marke of Tho Sheapard. Witnesses John Sampson, Robert Lambden. Recorded 20th Sept. 1653.
An Agreemt betweene Tho Sheapard & Mr fflynt	A long agreement regarding the boundry and future sale of the foregoing 75 acres. Dated 20th Sept. 1653. Signed Tho Sheapard his Marke, Ri fflynt. Witnesses: Tho Broughton, John Sampson. Recorded 20th Sept. 1653.
David Spiller his acknowledgmt - Robt Lambdon	"Whereas it hath been reported That I David Spiller have spoken words defamatory and aspercious against Robert Lambdon in saying that Jahe'l the wife of Willm Allen was the said Robert Lambson his whore and that I the said Spiller would prove it I doe therefore hereby acknowledge that in soe saying I have done the said Lambdon appalent and eminent wrong and I am no wayes Capable to Justify as being altogether unknowing and ignorant of any such matter As witnes my hand the 17th day of Septem 1653 Signum David Spiller In the presence of Nicholas Morris John Haynie Jeffery Goche The mke of Wm Spicer 20 Septem 1653 This acknowledgmt was Recorded "

Record Book #14. page 34.

James Claughton his sale of two Cowes to Jo'n Powell	Bill of sale for two cows dated 20th Sept. 1653. Signed James Claughton. Witnesses: Ger Dodson, Thomas Philpott. Recorded 20 Sept. 1653.
Tho Dunkington his Indenture to Everard Roberts	"This Indenture made the first day of Novem in the year of our Souveraigne Lord the King and in the year 1649 betweene me Everard Roberts of the one party and Thomas Dunkington of the other". Thomas Dunkington binds himself to serve Roberts 6 years. Signed The marke of Tho Dunkington. Everard Roberts. Witness John ffoster.
Everard Roberts his Assignmt of an Indenture to Rich Holden	Roberts assigns foregoing to Holden. Dated 14 May 1652. Signed Everard Roberts. Witnesses: Hen Hailes, James Willis. Date of record destroyed.
Hugh Lee his sale of a Cow to Marga Bashaw	Bill of sale dated 17th Sept 1653. Signed Hugh Lee. Witnesses: Henry Rooke, Robert Tuck (?) Recorded 20 Sept. 1653.

Record Book #14. page 34.

Wm Clapham his lre of Attur to Wm Thomas	Power of Atty. Wm Clapham to "my loving friend Wm Thomas" to receive debts from Richard fflynt. Dated 11th Aug. 1653. Signed with a mark. Witnesses: John Cornish, Edward Coles. Recorded 20th Sept. 1653.
Tho Hawkins his lre of Attur to Wm Thomas	Power of Atty. Hawkins to "my loving friend Wm Thomas" to collect debts. Dated 22 June 1653. Signed Thomas Hawkins, Witness Gabriel Odyer. Recorded 20 September 1653.
John Davies his Depo	Entry mutilated. "John Davies aged 25 yeares or thereabouts being sworne and examined saith That this Depont was with Mr Lee at John Danbys in Maryland when he was arrested and that Mr - - - - to put in Richard Span and an other for security - - - John Danby denied and then Mr Lee gott Mr Joseph Maning to pay Tobco there for him wch he promised to pay on this side againe ffurther saith not John Davies his mke Jurat in Cur 20 Septem: 1653".

Record Book #14. page 35.

Gershon Cromwell his Depo	"Gershon Cromwell aged 43 years or thereabouts being sworne and examined saith That Thom- (Thomas Hailes ?) showing 2 hheads unto Passep an Indian told - - he would give him a Mack-Coate if he would - - them with corne for him and thereupon gave him a Mack coate to wch the said Passep agreed B- - - when he was to perform his promise he onely paid to the said Hailes 3 barrells of Corne or thereabouts whereupon the said Hailes was angry with him for not being as good as his word then the said Passep threatened to kill both this Depont and the said Hailes Whereupon this Depont turned him out of Doares and the said Hailes neither sett his doggs upon him nor beate him And further saith not Gershon Cromwell his mke 20 Sept 1653 Jurat in Cur".
Matthew Rhoden his Depo	"Matthew Rhoden aged 33 yeares or thereabouts being sworne and examined saith That he this Depont goeing to his owne house the last Court as this Depont remembers and talking with Wm Thomas about the suite betweene Capt Hackett and Mr Lee This Depont wished the said Thomas to agree it The said Thomas said he could not for I must be true whore I am interested for it is my living and I can'ot worke And further saith not Matthew Rhoden 20 Septem 1653 Jurat in Cur".
Collo Mottrom his Accot upon Mr Suningberks estate	"The Accompt of Colo John Mottrom Ad'tor of all and singular the Goods and Chattels of Mr fflorentine Siningberk late whilest he lived in the parish of Chickacone in the County of Northumberland in the Colony of Virginia decd taken the 20th of Septem 1653". a/c total s 6526 lb. tobo. Recorded 20 Sept 1653.

Record Book #14. page 35

John Cooke	An Inventory of John Cooks estate.	
his Inventory	Totals 9619 pounds of tobacco.	
	Includes the following items:	

```
more one old Bible and 5 old books                    0050
more 1 old doublet and Capp                           0050
more 1 Bill of Corbet Pedell and Tho Rice             0600
more 28 Armslength of Ryanoke                         0114
more one Bill of ffrancis Grayes                      0300
more for 1 old cow bobtailed                          0400
```
   Inventory signed Alexander Baynham
                        Hercules Bridges
Recorded 20 Sept. 1653.

Note: So one old bob-tailed cow was worth 8 Bibles and forty books. And as for the Indian coin, we wonder what the squaws who made it thought of that price, but then of course they did not think.   B.F.

Record Book #14. page 36.

Mr Pope his Account
upon John Cooks estate
                       John Cooke Debtor

```
Imprs paid to Mr John Hallowes                        1100
paid to Robert Cole                                   0430
paid to Mr Hillard                                    0700
paid to Mr Hallowes for Abraham Moone                 0865
paid to Mr Speke                                      0300
paid to Rich: Hills                                   0060
paid due to Nathaniel Pope                            0467
paid Abraham Moone                                    0450
paid to John Jenkins to finish worke due from
            John Cooke                                0600
paid for Country Levies                               0500
  - Edward Ryalls                                     0100
more due to Nathaniel Pope                            0558
paid to Mr Gerrard                                    1000
paid to Mr Brodhurst                                  0100
paid to Henry Brooks                                  0250
paid for 11 gallons sacke                             0440
paid for his burial charges                           0600
paid for the praiseing of the estate                  0200
paid  the Clerks fees                                 0222
     x x x                                              -
                                                     ----
    Recorded 20 Sept 1653.                            9542
```

Mr Conyers his Release of Land to Mr Sam Smith	Thomas Conyers releases land to Smith as a loan. Dated 1 March 1652/3. Signed Tho Conyers. Witnesses: The marke of Henry Barnes, James Roper. Recorded 22 Sept. 1653.

115

Record Book #14. page 36.

Mr Hollowes his Depo	"John Hollowes gent aged 40 yeares or thereabouts being sworne and examined saith That he this Depont heard Mr Dodson confess at Mr Dedmans house that his the said Dodsons Instruments were false - - they were tryed at Colonel Claybornes And further this Depont saith not Jo Hollowes 21 Octo 1653 Jurat in Cur Westmorlandias "
Mr Dedman his Depo	"John Dedman gent aged 30 yeares or thereabouts being sworne and examined saith The very same verbatim that Mr Hollowes hath deposed and further saith not John Dedman (or Dodman) 21 Octo 1653 Jurat in Cur Westmorlandis "

Record Book # 14. page 37. This page torn.

Mrs Speke   Entry mutilated. "Ann the wife of Tho Speke gent
her Depo   aged 42 years or thereabouts being sworne and examined saith - - - Mr Winter Chapman brought into this Country - - servants about 4 or 5 years ago to sell - - them to this Deponts husbands house Amon- - were two boys named Henry and Thomas West - - were brothers and the older was bound by Indenture to serve 5 yeares the other wch was the younger Though no Indenture was signed by the said boy yet she this Depont heard the said boy say - - consent that he was to serve Colo John Mo- (Mottrom) 7 yeares and for soe long time the said Colo - Mottrom bought him and further this Depont saith not Ann Speke   4 Novem 1653 Jurat Coram me Walt'o Brodhu- (Brodhurst) "

George Day   "George Day aged 23 yeares or thereabouts being
his Depo   sworne and examined saith That this Depont came in the shipp with Mr Winter Chapman about 4 or 5 years agoe when the said Mr Chapman brought in two boys that were brotheren the elder   of them named Henry was to serve by Indenture 5 yeares and the younger named Thomas West was to serve for 7 yeares and this Depont heard the said Thomas say that he was to serve 7 yeares in the Country And that Colo John Mottrom bought the said Henry and Thomas of the said Mr Chapman and further saith not   George Day his marke 29 Octo 1653 Jurat Coram me Tho Speke "

Mr Speke   "Thomas Speke gent aged 30 yeares or thereabouts
his Depo   being sworne and examined saith That Mr Winter Chapman" -etc. The same data shown in his wife's deposition. Signed Tho Speke. Dated 4th November 1653.

Caption torn   "Cuthbert ffelpe aged 29 yeares or thereabouts
away   being sworne and examined saith that he this Depont coming out of Virginia as a Passenger in Mr Hen Rooke his shallop whereof John Squibb was the skipper & goeing into Horne harbour to finde some house for shelter and accomodacon Wee came to a house the doore being open and none inhabitting in it & there made a fire & quartered all night & continued - (2 ?) dayes While this Depont and the rest of the company were there came Mr Hall and his wife & the company craveing leave of him to continue in the house wch was granted & he said he had the disposing of the house and that they were
(continued on next page)

Record Book #14.   page 37.

The Deposition of Cuthbert ffelpe-continued.

welcome Afterward the wind setting faire this Depont and John Squibb
came aboard and left John Tingey his wife and family in the house and
when they came aboard the said Tingey was asked by some of the company
whether he had put out the fire that was in the house that it would
doe no harme He Answered yes and soe the shallop set saile and when
they were 4 or 5 miles off from the house They saw the house on fire
but how it came or who sett it on fire this Depont knoweth not
Saveing that John Tingey & his family were last in the house and furth'
this Depont saith not   Cuthbert ffelp   4 Novem 1653 Jurat Coram me
Tho Speke".

Mr Rich Cole   Cole registers mark for cattle 8 Nov. 1653.
his marke

John Stanley   John Stanley of the County of Northumberland,
his sale to   planter, sells certain cattle to Tho Orlye of the
Tho Orlye   same County, planter. Dated 7th Nov. 1653.
                       Signed John Stanlie his marke. Witnesses: Ralph
                       Horsly his mke, Isaac Knight. Rec. 12 Nov. 1653.

Record Book #14.   page 38.

Tho Orlye   Orlye registers mark for cattle 12 Nov. 1653.
his marke

David Phillipps   David Phillipps of Appomattacks in the County of
his Assignmt to   Westmorland assigns to Mr. Richard Turney "all my
Mr Turney   right title & interest of this writeing here
                       specified". Entry does not state what this writing
is. Dated 28th Sept. 1653. Signed David Phillipps. Witnesses: The
marke of Richard Browne, - - Baynham. Recorded 20 October 1653.

John Mottrom   Grant. Sir William Berkeley to John Mottrom 250
his pattent   acres commonly called the widow H- - Thickett, on
                       the Potomack River, near the land of George
Colclough. This land assigned Mottrom by Justinian Tennis, who had it
for the transportation of 5 persons into the colony. Dated 18 Dec.1650.

Colo Mottrom his   Entry mutilated. About 1/3 gone. Appearing upon the
Assignmt of this   remaining fragments: - " -hn Mottrom Junr bearing
Pattent to Mr   date the first day - - 1650 on the backside of the
Colclough   survey". This entry is dated 29 of Sept 1653. The
                       signature torn away. Witnessed by "Th Wilsford
No'ry Publick" and following that "12 Novem 1653 This Assignmt was
acknowledged in Court unto Mr Geo Colclough by Collo Mottrom and the
Assignmt & Pattent are Recorded".

Caption   Thomas Hailes sells 200 acres, recorded on page 32
destroyed.   of this book, to John Tingey. Dated 22 Nov. 1653.
                       Signed Tho Hailes his marke. Witnesses Tho Kedby,
                       Tho Hawkins. Recorded 22 Nov. 1653.

117

Record Book #14. page 38.

Abraham Byram his Assignmt - John Essex his Pattent to Gerveys Dodson	Byram assigns to Gervayse Dodson, surveyor, "within mentioned Land and Pattent". Dated 19 Nov. 1653. Signed Abraham Byram his mark. Witnesses: Robert Lambdon, Peter Knight. Recorded 21 Nov. 1653.
Caption destroyed.	Entry mutilated. It is a patent from Sir William Berkeley. The name Timothy Lodell appears twice in the fragments. The patent is dated 15 Sept. 1651. This patent may have been issued to Timothy Lodell and Thos. Broughton.

Record Book #14. page 39.

Tho Broughton his Assignmt of a Pattent to Tho Ellis	Entry stained and mutilated. I cannot read it. Upon fragments appear the date 21 Nov. 1653. It is signed Tho Brough-. The Witnesses are Phillip Carpenter, Henry Cartwright. Recorded 21 Nov 1653.
John - -(Rocke ?) & Wm Newman their Pattent	A patent from Sir William Berkeley. The balance of the entry gone entirely.
Caption missing.	Entry altogether destroyed.
John - - his sale Goo - -	Mutilated. The name John Meekes appears on fragments. Dated 21 Nov. - -. Signed "The marke of John Meekes". Witnesses, gone. Then "21 Novem 1651 (sic) This sale was acknowledged in Court - George Knott- - John Meekes- - was Recorded".
- - Sharpe - sale of Land - Anthony (appears to be Linton)	Entry practically destroyed. Upon fragments "That I Ro Sharpe of the parish of Harrop James Citty County" and the date 1652.
Antho Li- assignmt - to - -	Entry practically destroyed. the name Anthony Linton appears on fragments and the date 21 Nov. 1653. And "was acknow- in Court unto Geo Knott by Anthony Lin- - - is Recorded".

Record Book #14. page 40.

Mr Broughton his sale of Land to Mr Colclough — Thomas Broughton of Northumberland Co., gent., sells to George Colclough of the same Co., gent., half of a tract of land granted to him (Broughton) called Hulls Thickett, of 420 acres. Dated 21 Nov. 1653.
Signed Tho Broughton. Witnesses: John Hall, Wm Wildey, Hen J- -.
Recorded 21st Nov. 1653.

Record Book #14. page 40.

Joseph Wicks
his lre of Attur

"Know all men by these presents That I Joseph Wicks of the Isle of Kent doth institute appoint and ordaine my trusty & welbeloved friend Nicholas Morris gent of Great Wicocomocoe in Virginia to sue and impleade David Spiller for me & in my name". Last of the entry mutilated and missing. The date 2 Oct. 1653 appears and the name of a witness, Wm Spicer. Recorded 21 Novem 165- (1653).

Wm Thomas
his lre of Attur

Power of Atty. to "loveing friend Abra Byram " regarding suits in the next Court. Dated 6th Nov. 1653. Signed Wm Thomas. No witnesses. Recorded 21 Nov. 1653.

Caption gone.

Mutilated. Power of Atty. Entry is dated 18th Nov. 1653. Signed Richard Cole. Witnesses: George Berry, Will -ered. "21 No 1653 This lre of attur was Recorded".

Mr Speke his
lre of Attur

Power of Atty. Thomas Speke gent of Nominye to John W- - to transact business in Northumberland Court on Nov. 20th. Dated 20 Nov. 1653. Signed Tho Speke. Witness Walter Brodhurst. Recorded 20 Sept 1653 (sic)

Edward Henley
his Depo

"Edward Henley aged 33 yeares or thereabouts being sworne and examined saith That about the latter end of this last sum'er he this Depont heard a Dogg Soloing of a hogg in Mr Wilsfords Corne ground feareing the hogg might come into this Deponts corne stept out to the swamp to provent his comeing over he heard some beating of the said hogg while the dogg sole'd him presently after came Wm Allenson & John Davies to the swampe side & spoke to this Depont that the dogg sh- - - him no more for they had given - - - Boare his supper he might goe to - - to that effect Since wch time the Depont never saw the said Boare and further saith not Edw Henley his marke 17th 9 ber 1653 Jurat Coram me John Mottrom 21 9 ber 1653 This Depo was Recorded".

Joane Henley
her Depo

"Joane Henley aged 28 yeares or thereabouts being sworne and examined saith That" . This entry badly damaged. Apparantly about the same as the foregoing regarding the hog in Mr. Wilsford's corn. Dated 17th 9 ber 1653.

Record Book #14. page 41.

John Dennis
his Depo

Badly torn and remaining fragments stained. "John Dennis aged 3- (this appears to be either 34 or 35 but it is impossible to state positively) yeares or thereabouts - - (two lines destroyed here)- - house- - Bed - - house made a fire - - - this Depont abord for John Squibb & Cuthbert - - and there continueing about 5 dayes this Depont carried Squibb and Cuthbert aborde leaveing Tingey & his family in the said house wch he afterward carryed aborde and further this Depont saith that there was a fire made without doores but with snow & raine was p- - 3 dayes before their departure from the house ffurther saith not John Davies his marke 21 9 ber 1653 Jurat in Cur ".

Record Book #14. page 41.

Tho Coggin / his Depo
"The Deposition of Tho Coggin aged 26 yeares or thereabouts sworne and examined saith That being at the house of Mr Nicholas Morris he heard Mr Calvert call Richard Budd Churchrobber & a Rogue & Theefe & that he would prove him a Rogue & further saith not The marke of Tho Coggin : Nicho Morris 21 9ber 1653 This Depo was Recorded".

David Spiller / his Depo
"The Deposition of David Spiller aged 34 yeares or thereabouts sworne and examined and saith That being at the house of Mr Nicholas Morris he heard Mr Calvert call Richard Budd Churchrobber & a Rogue & Theefe & that he would prove him a Rogue & further saith not The marke of David Spiller Nicho Morris 21 9ber 1653 This Depo was Recorded".

Wm Spicer / his Depo
"The Deposition of Wm Spicer aged 38 yeares or thereabouts sworne & examined & saith That he heard Mr Calv- - (Calvert) - - the wife of Richard Budd" This entry is mutilated. Not very nice words appear on the fragments. Signed Wm Spicer Nicholas Morris. "21 9ber 1653 this Depo was Recorded".

Moriall Margreg-gor / her Depo
Entry mutilated. "- - aged 34 yeares or there- -" Signed Mer- - - egger Nicholas Morris. "21 9ber 1653 This Depo: was Recorded".

Caption gone. It is however: John Walton, his Depo.
Opening words of entry gone. "- - Mr Joseph Maning - - - Selliaks name - - - to be paid to any one of them and that Maning was Arrested in Virginia by Selliaks And further saith not John Walton his marke 21 9ber 1653 Jurat in Cur".

- - Hawkins - Depo
"Thomas Hawkins aged 35 yeares or thereabouts being sworne and examined saith that he this Depont being by when Mr Presly bought some servants sugar & shoes of Mr Husbands he this Depont never heard Mr Husbands name any Cashe to be paid by the said Mr Presly with his Tobco and further saith not Tho Hawkins 21 9ber Jurat in Cur".

Mr Morris / his Depo
"Mr Nicholas Morris aged 48 yeares or thereabouts being sworne and examined saith That he hath heard Mrs Calvert say that she dare not goe out with Mr Calvert her husband into the woods or into private for feare he would kill her & he hath seene Mr Calvert halle her into private but she would not goe with him He this Depont doth verily beleeve that the words spoken agt the States were spoken by her onely to seave & protect her from the furye of her husband that she might be taken into safe Custody & be parted from her husband and further saith not Nicholas Morris". No date on the record. Evidently the same as the other depositions regarding the Calverts.

Note: And verily I still do not beleeve or trust Mr. Morris. B.F.

Record Book #14.   page 41.   (this page mutilated)

Mr Hallowes his lre of Attur	Power of Atty. Mr John Hallowes to John Walton. Dated 5th Novem - -. Signed John Hallowes. Witness: - Sampson or Simpson. Rec. 21 9ber 1653.
John Essex & - Hurst - - of Attur	Entry mutilated. "We John Essex & Henry Hurst doe appoint Abraham - - ". Dated 18th day of - - -. Signed John Essex his marke Henry - -. Witness: - - Lambdon. Recorded 21 Nov. 1653.

Record Book #14.   page 42.

Hen Rayner his marke — Henry Rayner of Northumberland Co. registers mark for cattle and hogs 28th Nov. 1653.

Wm Hopkins his marke — Wm Hopkins of Northumberland Co., registers mark for cattle and hogs 28th Nov. 1653.

Wm Medcalfe his marke — Wm Medcalfe of Northumberland Co., registers mark for cattle and hogs 1st December 1653.

Wm Beesly his Depo — "William Beesly aged 22 yeares or thereabouts being sworne and examined saith That he this Depont came into this Colony of Virginia in the shipp called the Honor in wch ship came one Vincent Cox servant to Mr Bullocke and the said shipp came to anchor in Virginia about the 8th or the 10th day of October last was fower yeares and further this Depont saith not Wm Beesly his marke"

John Drap (sic) his Depo — "John Draper (sic) aged 22 yeares or thereabouts being sworne and examined saith the very same that his coatest (cotestant) Wm Beesly hath deposed verbatim And further saith not The marke of John Drap (sic). 17 Decem 1653 Jurat fuerant Coram me Walter Brodhurst ".

Entries for the year 1654 begin here.

Walter Pakes his Acquittance to Mr Simpson — A long entry badly stained. Pakes releases "Paul Simpson Gent late of the Province of Mary-Land in America" from all obligations to him. Dated 3 Jan. 1653/4. Signed Walter Pakes. Witnesses: Tho Wilsford Notary Public, Bridgett Wilsford. Rec. 25 Jan 1653/4

John Stanley his sale of Cattle to John Knight — Mr John Stanley of the Co. of Northumberland, Planter sells certain cattle to John Knight of the same place planter. Dated 7th Nov. 1653. Signed John Stanley his marke. Witness Ralph Horsly his marke. Recorded 30th January 1653/4.

John Knight his Assignmt of Cattle to Tho Orley — Knight assigns foregoing cattle to Orley. Dated 31st December 1653. Signed John Knight. Witnesses Tho Broughton, Geo Courtnell his marke. Recorded 30th January 1653/4.

121

Record Book #14. page 42.

Mr Turney his acquitt to Tho Wilsford	"20 Octo 1653 Recd of Tho Wilsford 330 lb of tobco in full for order of Court dated 20th Sept 1653 wch tobacco was attached in his hand for the debt of Mr Wm Knight. Signed Richard Turney. Witness John Sampson. Recorded 31 Jan. 1653/4.

Record Book #14. page 43.

Robert Bradshaw his sale of a Cow to Tho Wilsford	Robert Bradshaw of Northumberland Co., sells a cow and calf to Wilsford. Dated 1 Jan 1653/4. Signed Robert Bradshaw. Recorded 31 Jan. 1653/4.
Capt Jo: Smith his pattent	Patent. Sir William Berkeley to Capt. John Smith 200 acres in Northumberland Co., on NW side of Chicacone bordering another tract of land of Capt. Jno. Smith, for transp. of 4 persons into the colony. Dated 16 Sept.1651.
Capt Smith his Assignment to Wm Cocke	Capt John Smith of Wicocomocoe assigns right in foregoing to Wm Cocke. Dated 23 Feb. 1651/2. Signed John Smith. Witness Bartholomew Bloome.
Colo Mottrom his Assignmt to Edm Singclere and Edm Edwards	Entry damaged. Half missing. John Mottrom apparently assigns all interest in the administration of the estate of - - - to Edmund Singclere and Edmund Edwards. A date appears, 16 ffeb 1653, but whether this is the date of assgnmt or date of record is uncertain.
Tho Gaskins & David Spiller their gift to Jane Allen	Entry badly damaged. Gaskins and Spiller give to Jane Allen w- (wife ?) of Wm Allen two cows. Recorded 16 ffeb 1653/4.
Caption gone.	Ralph Horsley of Northumberland County in Virginia, planter, "doe out of the naturall love and affection wch I bear to my only sone Joseph Horsley" gives a cow and a calf. The male increase to revert to him (Ralph) until Joseph attains the age of 21. Dated 3rd Jan. 1653/4. Signed Ralph Horsley. Witnesses: Geo Colclough, Hugh Lee. Ack. and Rec. 16 Feb. 1653/4.

Hugh Lees agreement with Robert Sharpe — Hugh Lee and Robert Sharp, both of Northumberland Co., agree that Lee goes security for debts of Sharpe, amounting to 3889 lb. tobo, he (Sharpe) giving his crop as security to Lee. Entry damaged and part missing. Debts appear to be:

to Wm Neuman	300
Mr Trussell	4-9
Richard Hills	23-
- - ffoster	200

Dated - 1653. Signed - - - Hugh Lee. Witnesses: - -. John Barnes. Date of record gone.

Tho Kingwell his gift to Eliza West	Entry damaged. Tho Kingwell appoints Robert Lambdon to receive a heifer 2 yeares old. Balance of entry illegible. Recorded 16th Feb. 1653/4.

Record Book #14. page 44.

John Davies his lre of Attur to Nathan Hickman	Power of Atty. John Davies to Nathaniel Hickman to collect debts from Thomas Wilsford. Dated - Feb. 1653/4. Signed The marke of John Davies. Witness, the Marke of Wm Allen. Rec 16 Feb. 1653/4.
Mr Simpson his lre of Attur to Tho Wilsford	Entry damaged. Part gone. Power of Atty. Paul Simpson (or Sampson) to Tho Wilsford. Dated 8th Feb. -. Signed Pa Simpson. Witness, The marke of Wm Greensted. Recorded 16 Feb. 1653/4.
Tho Sheapard his lre of Attur to John Powell	Entry damaged. Power of Atty. Thomas Sheapard to "my loving friend John Powell" regarding business, evidently the collection of debts from Thomas Hawkins, Mr John Hallowes and Seth ffoster. Date missing. Signed Tho Sheapard. Names of witnesses missing. Also date of record.
Eudward Roberts lre of Attur to Jo Earle	Entry mutilated. Power of Atty. Dated 6th February 1653/4. Signed Eudward Roberts. Witnesses, Daniel Roberts, The marke of John Walker. Rec. 16 Feb. 1653/4.
- - - his - - - to - - Vincent	Power of Atty. Richard Holden to Henry Vincent "in a cause depending betweene Eudward Roberts and myselfe". Dated 16 Feb. 1653. Signed the marke of Rich Holden. Recorded 16th Feb. 1653/4.
Wm Allen his -itt to David Spiller	David Spiller publicly acknowledges before Mr Richard Budd & Gervase Dodson that he is sorry "for any words that he hath in his drincke or otherwyse at any time spoken tending to the defamation of Jane Allen" the wife of Wm Allen. Allen agrees to release him from arrest and damages. Dated 18th of Nov.--. Signed Wm Allen. Witnesses, John Wife (Wise ?), Richd Budd. Recorded 16 Feb. 1653/4.
Jane Allen her acquittance to David Spiller	Jane Allen, wife of Wm Allen, acquits Spiller. Dated - Nov. 1653. Signed The marke of Jane Allen. Witnesses: -Haynie, John Wife. Rec. 16 Feb. 1653/4.
Tho Gerrard his Depo	Entry damaged. Thomas Gerrard (part of entry showing age missing) makes a deposition regarding hogs. Refers to having lived with Mr. Nicholas Morris. Signed Tho Garrard his marke. Dates missing.
John Walker his marke	John Walker of Northumberland registers mark for cattle and hogs 16th Feb. 1653/4.

Record Book #14. page 45.

Mr Hallowes his Depo him and Mr Selleake further saith not landis".	"John Hallowes gent aged 38 yeares or thereabouts sworne & examined saith that Mr Chichester tolde this De- - - Mr Joseph Maning - - sell goods for - -bills for paymt of tobco to any one of them and John Hallowes 20 ffeb 1653 Jurat in Cur Westmor-

Record Book #14. page 45.

James Reynolds his marke	James Reynolds of Northumberland Co., registers mark for cattle and hogs 18th March 1653. (1653/4)
Wm Reynolds Junr his marke	Wm Reynolds Junr., of Northumberland Co., registers mark for cattle and hogs 18th March 1653/4.
Robert Sharpe his marke	Robert Sharpe of Northumberland Co., registers his mark for cattle and hogs 20 March 1653/4.
Edw Henley his marke	Edwd Henley of Northumberland Co., registers his mark for cattle and hogs 20th March 1653/4.
Eudward Roberts his acquittance to Hen Haler	Roberts acquits Haler (Hales ?) from all debts including "Mr Jones Bill & Mr Lewis his Bill". Dated 13th May 1654. Signed Eudward Roberts. Witnesses: Richard Holdens mke, James Willis mke. Recorded 20 March 1653/4.
Walter Weekes his gift to Walter Allenson	Walter Weekes of Northumberland gives a calf to Walter Allenson. Dated 20 May 1654. Witness Hen Toppin his mke. Recorded 20 May 1654.
- - Quart'r - - Mr Presly Sherr	"At a Quarter Court held at James Citty the 14th of March 1653 Present Richard Bennett Esq Govern'r Col Claiborne Coll Higginson Coll Pettus Coll Geo Ludlow Leift Coll ffreeman Coll Wm Taylor Esq

Mr Wm Presly is by the Governor and Court nominated and Chosen high Sheriff of the County of Northumberland & to be sworn next County Court held there   Teste Ro Hubard Cl Cour   20 May 1654 This Ord'r was Recorded".

- Thomas Attur - Michael his -ent of a Pattent Coles	Entry stained and blurred. Wm Thomas, Attorney of John Michael, assigns right in patent to Richard Coles. Dated 20 July 1654. Signed Wm Thomas.
Rob: Vaulx his lre of Attur to Mr Broughton	Power of Atty. Robert Vaulx, merchant, to "my welbeloved friend Tho Broughton" to collect tobacco, beaver or any other commodities in the counties of Lancaster, Northumberland and Westmorland. Dated

29th June 1654. Signed Robt Vaulx. Witnesses Charles Edmunds his mke, Christopher Roberts. Recorded 20 July 1654.

Record Book #14. page 46.

John Smith his gift of a Calfe to Wm Smith	Mutilated. The connection betw. John and Robert does not show, that part of record missing. "Know all men by these presents That I John Smith - - Robert Smith for the naturall love and affection that I -

unto my brother William Smith doe freely give my said brother William one Cowe calfe x x". Dated 20 July 1654. Signed John Smith his mark. Witnesses Robert Smith, Th Wilsford. Recorded 20 July 1654.

Record Book #14. page 46.

Mary Playce her gift to her Children	"Whereas Mary Playce in her widowhood did give unto John Playce her sone one yearling heifer" and certain other cattle. This cattle not being recorded, Mary Playce "in the presence of Mr Peter Knight and John Gresham her then late husband upon her bed being sicke she the said Mary then being the wife of John Gresham did desire her said husband Gresham that whereas the said cattle as then not Recorded for the use of the said John Playce her sone she the said Mary then giving one brendled yearling heifer being of the said stocke and marke unto Justinian Gresham her youngest sone x x ". Dated 20 July 1654. Signed John Gresham. Witnesses: Wm Presly, Tho Bales his marke.
Wm Light his lre of Attur to James Macgreggor	Power of Atty. Light to Macgreggor to sue and recover a Bill of 600 lb. tobo. from Mr John Mottrom Esq. Dated 20 Feb. 1653/4. Signed William Light. Witness Rob Lee. Recorded 20 July 1654.
- - ough his - - Jo: Compton - - Bedlam	George Colclough gives to John Compton Junior a cow of John Mottrom's mark. Also a calf. Dated 20 July 1654. Signed Geo Colclough. Rec. 20 July 1654.
Wm Botts his sale of Land to John Motley	Botts sells to Motley 200 acres in Great Wicococomo River, adj. land of Colo. Claiborne and Edward Coles. Dated 20 July 1654. Signed William Botts. Witnesses George Colclough, Hugh Lee. Rec. 20 July 1654.
Mar..in Cole his sale of Land to John Rodford	Martin Cole of Northumberland, Planter, sells to John Rodford, Gent., 160 acres on the north side of Wicococomoco river, adj. land of Geo Wale (or Hale). This land granted to Cole 5th Oct. 1653. This sale dated 20 July 1654. Signed Martin Cole his marke. Witnesses: Tho Kedby, Tho Wilsford. Recorded 20 July 1654. The above name may be Redford, Rodford or Radford. It is impossible to say which it is in this entry.

Record Book #14. page 47.

Wm Presly his gift to ffrances Mottrom	Wm Presly gives a calf to Frances the daughter of Col. John Mottrom, "she being my wifes Goddaughter". Dated 20 July 1654. Signed William Presly. Recorded 20th July 1654.
Hugh Lee his gift of a yearling to Wm Bedlam	Hugh Lee gives a heifer to Wm Bedlam, Junior. Dated 4th March 1653/4. Signed Hugh Lee. Witnesses Matthew Rhoden, George Colclough. Recorded 20th July 1654.
Tho Hayles his pattent	Grant. Sir William Berkeley to Tho Hayles, 300 acres in Northumberland on S. side of Potomac River, adj. land of George Knott, Edward Walker and John Powell. Dated 18th September 1651. Signed Wm Berkeley.

Record Book #14. page 47.

Tho Hayles his Assignmt of a Pattent to Rob: Lord	Foregoing patent assigned to Robert Lord. Dated 20 July 1654. Signed Tho Hayles his mke. Witness Th Wilsford. Recorded 21 July 1654.
Caption torn away	Anthony Linton of Northumberland, planter, "in consideration of my naturall Love and affection to my dear sister Alice Shaw wife of Thomas Shaw now

of Yorke County" gives them 250 acres, "being the uppermost of my Dividend". Dated "this last of August 1653". Signed Anthony Linton his marke. Witnesses Ger Dodson, John Thackle (?). Rec. 20 July 1654.

Mr Rogers his gift to his children	John Rogers of Northumberland in the Colony of Virginia, Gent., for natural love and affection for his children gives them as follows: "my Daughter Katherine Rogers" a calf. to Elizabeth Rogers a calf. to John Rogers a calf.

Dated 20 July 1654. Signed John Rogers. Witness, Th Wilsford Not'y Pubck. Recorded 20th July 1654.

Rob: Sharpe his Depo	Entry damaged. "Robert Sharpe aged 40 yeares or thereabouts being sworne and examined saith That he this Depont was at Tho Shaws house with Mr Pew

& Anthony Linton demanded that he might have the benefit of the Peach trees according to the - - - - them Tho Shaw had him share them and - - them away according to his promise or else he would cutt them up and if Mr Radford came - - he would breake his tubbs that the coop should not - - again and further saith not Robert Sharpe 20 July 1654 Jurat in Cur".

Record Book #14. page 48.

John Davies his Depo	"John Davies aged 36 yeares or thereabouts being sworne and examined saith The very same that Robert Sharpe hath deposed and further saith not John Davies his marke 20 July 1654 Jurat in Cur".
Rob: Smith his marke	Smith records his mark for cattle and hogs 20th July 1654.
More Com'rs Nominated	"Collo Mottrom Mr Samuel Smith hath signified - - - to have some more nominated for Com'rs in the Court for the better disposal of busines Wherefore

you are hereby authorized to sweare for Com'rs Mr Richard Cole Mr James Hawley and Mr Wm Reynolds and that Mr Sam Smith be of the Quorum Dated the 29th of July 1654 Ri Bennett   Wm Claiborne".

Record Book #14. page 48.

John Ingram his Will	Will of John Ingram of Great Wicocomocoe in the County of Northumberland. To my daughter Elizabeth Ingram, a bed and furniture and cattle when she shall be 18 years old. To my oldest son, Thomas Ingram, horses, cows, bed and the land "I now live on at the Dividing Creek excepting 100 acres that Tho Brewer now liveth upon to Tho Hopkins forever". To son Thomas "2 pewter dishes one dozen of spoons Chamberpott and Iron pott of five gallons one pewter drinking pott two fowleing peeces one new saddle and bridle one Iron pestle of 40 lbs weight one man servant for fower or five yeares to serve". To my daughter Jane Ingram 330 acres, a bed, etc. To loving wife Jane Ingram the remainder of the estate. "my oldest sone Thomas for to be brought up to read & wright". "That Tho Hopkins shall live during his life or as long as he pleases in the same manner as he did when I lived that is he is for to have one roome in my house to himselfe & meate drink washing & lodging & not be interrupted by aney". "Mr Wm Nash Mr Peter Knight and Mr Thomas Hopkins for to see all things performed according my desire". Dated 8th April 1654. Signed John Ingram. Witnesses: Ger Dodson, Robert Burrell, Thomas Brewers marke. Proved 20 November 1654.
Wm Thomas his Bill of sale to Tho Salisbury	Thomas sells cattle to Salisbury. End of entry too badly stained to read. The date 1654 appears and the signature, Wm Thomas.

Record Book #14. page 49.

Wm Thomas his bill of sale - - Tho Salisbury	"Wicococomocoe July the 15 1653". Thomas sells Salisbury other cattle. Signed Wm Thomas. Witnesses: Rob:Sharpe, Hen Wicker. Rec.20 Nov.1654.
Mr Knight his gift to Thomas Prichett Junr	"x x I Peter Knight in consideration of my love unto Thomas Pritchett Junr" gives a heifer. Dated 7th November 1654. Signed Peter Knight. Witnesses Wm Spicer his marke, Geo Marsh. Rec. 20 Nov. 1654.
Mr Knight his gift to Thomas Waddy	"x x I Peter Knight in consideration of my love unto Thomas Waddy" gives a calf. Dated 17 Nov.1654. Signed Peter Knight. Witnesses: Rob Yeo, Daniel ffoxcroft. Recorded 20 Nov. 1654.
Caption mutilated.	John Rogers and George Trewett of Northampton Co., mortgage 5 cows to - - Weaver. Dated 30 May 1654. Signed John Rogers, George Trewitt. Witnesses: Wm Little, Tho Hopkins. Recorded 20th Nov. 1654.
Mr Broughtons agreem with Mr fflynt	Richard fflynt acks, Jdgmt. to Robt Vaulx for 1200 lb tobo. Thomas Broughton, Atty. for Vaulx makes agreement for payment at 400 lb per year. Dated 20 November 1654. Signed Tho Broughton. Witness Th Wilsford. Recorded 20 Nov. 1654.

127

Record Book #14. page 49.

John Prosser his bill to Tho Brewer	John Prosser of Wicocomocoo, Joyner, agrees to make for Tho Brewer one table "seaven foote long and one forme suddenly and two Chaires and two joyned stooles the table to be two foote an halfe All this

works to be very good and merchantable due to be paid betweene the 15th of August and the last of January next and for the true performance I the said Prosser doe binde over to the said Brewer one Browne Cow x x" Dated the 15th of August 1654. Signed John Prosser. Witnesses John Gamlin, Tho Hopkins. Recorded 20 Nov. 1654.

Record Book #14. page 50.

Tho Wilsford his Pattent	Entry stained and blurred. Grant. Sir William Berkeley 250 acres on Perries Creek. "The said land being due unto Tho Wilsford by purchase of Hugh Lee

overseer of the Orphanes of John Perrey deceased as also by and for the transportation of five persons whose names are hereunder mencioned". Dated 10th Nov. 1651. Signature not shown. "Vera Copia eto Rec Rob Huberd Cl Cur".
John Browne, Jacob Napleton, Th Pulford, Jose Calfe, Isaac Harrison.

Tho Wilsford his Assignmt of a Pattent unto Edw Henley	Wilsford assigns above to Henley. Dated 20 Novem 1654. Signed Th Wilsford. No witnesses shown. Recorded 20 Nov. 1654. Entry marked "Void vide fol: 80".
Tho Wilsford his pattent	Grant. 26 acres in Northumberland Co. Dated 1 Aug. 1653. Signed Ri: Bennett, Wm Claiborne Secr.
Tho Wilsford his Assignmt of Land to Edw Henley	Above land assigned to Henley. Dated 20 Nov. 1654. Signed Th Wilsford. Recorded 20 Nov. 1654. Entry marked "Void vide fol 80:".
Edw Henley his - to Th Wilsford	"This Bill bindeth me Edward Henley of the County of Northumberland Planter". He agrees to pay "Tho Wilsford of the County of Westmorland Gent" 6000

lb tobo. upon the plantation which Henley has now bought of Wilsford. Dated 20 Nov. 1654. Signed Edward Henley his marke. Witnesses Wm Nash, Nicholas Morris. Recorded 20 November 1654.

Edw Henley making over his plantacon Cowes & Crop to Tho Wilsford	Henley guarantees pmt., giving security for plantation. Dated 20 Nov. 1654. Signed Edward Henley his mark. Witnesses Will Nash, Nocho Morris. Recorded 20 Nov. 1654.

Record Book #14. page 51.

Hen Moseley his Depo	Entry stained and mutilated. Appears to be in regard to the payment of a debt. "Henry Moseley aged 40 yeares or thereabouts". Signed Hen- - - his mark. "20 Novem 1654 Jurat in Cur".

Record Book #14. page 51.

John Hull
his Depo
"John Hull aged 39 yeares or thereabouts being sworne and examined saith That he this Depont bought of Tho Bre- a yearling heifer if this Depont did like her when he saw her at Yorke when he came to Yorke he found - - heifer of the same marke and Culler that the said Brewer had sett downe in his bill of sale to this Depont and whe- this Depont had taken her into his ground at Colon- - - Taylor forwarned this Depont for medling with her - - gave ffrancis Hansworth Ordr to drive her out of this Deponts ground and to putt her with in the said Colonel - - - - force and further said that the said Brewer had unjustly marked her and unjustly came by her and further saith not   John Hull 20 Novem 1654 Jurat in Cur".

Rich Holdens sale
of Land to
Rob Laud
Holden sells Laud 50 acres being part of a tract of land formerly divided betw "me the said Holding & John Walker". Dated 2 Aug 1654. Signed Rich Holding. Witnesses, Wm Thomas, Hen Hayler. Ackn. in Court by Richd Holding 20 Aug. 1655.

Record Book #14. page 51. Begins year 1655.

Caption
mutilated
Bill binding Peircy Hamon and John Bradshaw to pay to Tho Wilsford 2000 lb. tobo. Dated 19 January 1652. Signed Peircy Hamon, John Bradshaw. Witnesses: Rich Titherton, Nathaniel Hickman. Recorded 20 Janu 1654. (1654/5).

Caption
illegible
"Let noe will be proved if any be made nor Administracon granted of the estate of Wm Ginsey late of the County of Northumberland deceased till Wm Warde Principall Creditor to the decd be first called   ffirst March 1654 This Caveat was entered". (1654/5).

Jno Kent his
Lre of Atturney
to Jno Earle
Power of Atty John Kent, planter, to John Earle, planter, to receive from Hugh Lee, Taylor, payment of bond dated 13 March 1653. Dated 24 Feb. 1654/5. Signed John Kent. Witnesses: Suck: Bruster, Phillip Carpenter. Recorded 20 Aug. 1655.

Mary Sharpe
her Depo
"Mary Sharpe aged 23 yeares or thereabouts sworne and examined sayth That shee heard Alice Shaue saye to her husband you rogue I was forced to take a false oath agt my Brother to keepe my bones from being broken and further sayth not 20th August 1655 Jurat in cur".

Mary Earle
her Depo
"Mary Earle aged 36 yeares or thereabouts sworne & examined sayth That Francis Symons asked Mr Seth Foster for his Bill the said Foster told him when hee came to Ralph Horsleys hee would give it him the - - - - for Mr Foster being decd before this - - - being at oyster shell point and further this depont sayth not   The mke of Mary Earle 20 August 1655 Jurat in Cur".

Record Book #14.   page 52.

Geo Nott   "George Nott aged 36 yeares or thereabouts". This
his Depo   entry mutilated. The fragments indicate that it
has to do with the Shaw-Linton family broil. There
is something about Shaws threatening to box his brother-in-law's ears
and about Mrs Linton milking other people's cows that came upon her
plantation. The usual recriminations in such cases. Dated 20 Aug.1655.

Elizabeth Nott   Entry mutilated. "Elizabeth Nott aged 36 yeares or
her Depo   thereabouts sworne - - the same that George Nott
hath deposed and fur- - sayeth that Thomas Shawe
sd that Anth Linton - - - and stood upon an Iland till the sloope came
and to - - this Depont sayeth not   Elizab Nott her marke 20 August
1655 Jurat in Cur".

Geo Berry   "George Berry aged 32 yeares or thereabouts sworne
his Depo   and examined - - the same that George and Elizab:
Nott hath deposed and further sayeth not   George
Berry 20th August 1655 Jurat in Cur".

Mr Rich'd Wright "Richard Wright aged 22 yeares or thereabouts
his Depo   sworne - - - that Mr Cololough told this depont
after hee made - - - that hee was glad Coll
Mottrom had done what he had done - - - to his children for hee the
sd Mr Cololough sd hee - - - in a m- - - fudled and further this depont
sayeth that they were drinking -alf a daye just before the will was
made & further sayeth not Richd Wright 20 August 1655 Jurat in Cur".

Mr Dodson   "Gervase Dodson aged 34 yeares or thereabouts
his Depo   sworne and examined sayth that being at Antho
Lentons House the said Lenton haveing given a
- - of Land to his Brother in Law Thomas Shawe for lives as may appear
by a wrighting wch this depont was desired to drawe the sd Lenton
asked the said Shawe if hee liked the said writing whoe answered
Yes but by reas- - pay was short and being it was thought no difference
- - - - - betwixt Brothers: this depont sett not downe in wrighting
- - hee thin- - one thing agreed upon wch was the said Lenton should
- - - - benefitt for to that purpose of halfe the Peach trees upon the
said Land hee gave to his sd brother Shawe wch Thomas Shawe agreed
to - - anthony Lenton said hee desired or cared not for them - - - -
till hee had his owne trees growne up to bear or - - purpose - - the
best of this depont rememberance & further sayeth not   Ger Dodson
20 August 1655 Jurat in Cur".

Robt Evans   "Robert Evans aged 24 yeares or thereabouts sworne
his Depo   and examined sayeth that hee did heare Capt Budd
saye hee did not looke upon Hen Maye as a stranger
but that hee would give him hid Dyett and further this depont sayeth
not Robt Evans his mke   20 of August 1655 Jurat in Cur".

Thomas Reade   "Thomas Reade aged 29 yeares or thereabouts sworne
his Depo   and examined sayeth that he - heare Capt Budd saye
that he did not look upon Henry Mayes as a stranger
but he did intend to have given him his Dyett & further sayeth not
Thomas Read   20th August 1655 Jurat in Cur".

Record Book #14.   page 52.

Caption worn away.   "John Haynie aged 31 yeares or thereabouts sworne and examined sayeth That all the comendacons that ever hee heard of Alice Atkinson is that shee was a Whore and further this depon't sayeth not   John Haynie   20th August 1655 Jurat in Cur".

Note: If Alice is being commended then what, if you please, would be adverse criticism ?   B.F.

- - Grinsted   "William Grinsted aged 21 yeares or thereabouts
- Depo   sworne and examined sayeth that hee this depon't
                   had the opportunity to lay his hand upon the thigh
of Alice Atkinson her smock being betweene and further sayeth not
Wm Grinsted his marke   20th August 1655   Jurat in Cur".

- - Knight   "Peter Knight aged 35 yeares   or thereabouts sworne
his Depo   and examined saith That the generall report of
                   Alice Atkinson that hee ever heard was shee was an
ill liver and one that never would live with her husband but that
shee rather alwaies was desirous of absence from her husband then for
to live with him and further this Depont sayeth not   Peter Knight
20 August 1655 Jurat in Cur".

Note: The following entry, out of place in the book, is introduced since it is the keynote to others that are included. Any man of any experience can immediately read between the lines. If Dick Wright had just been prepared with a little ready cash, as a gentleman should have been, we would have been deprived of this enlightening glimpse of colonial life.
     The entry has been mutilated twice, in that the first name of Richard Wright has been scratched over with modern ink in an effort to destroy his identity. Knowing the first name to be Richard, the original is plainly visible beneath the erasure.   B. F.

Northumberland Co. Virginia. Record Book #14. page 56.

Alice Atkinson her   "August the 22th 1655. The examination of Alice
Examination   Atkinson shee this examin't sayeth That being in
                      company with Mrs Salisbury shee the sd M'ris
Salisbury carried this examin't into the company of Mr Richd Wright Mr
Clay James Aston & severall others in a short time the company depted

and this examin't & Mrs Salisbury left alone Mrs Salisbury sd shee
would goe to the Court & heare the cause tryed concerning Mr Morris
his maide & asked mee if I would goe with her this examin't replyed
& said shee was not very well but told her the sd Mris Salisbury
that if shee were any better shee would come imediately after Mris
Salisburys depture came Samuel Bonham w'th some wine & asked this
examin't where M'ris Salisbury was this examin't told him that shee
was gone to the Court to heare a Cause tryed concerning Mr Morris
his maide the said Bonham asked this examin't if he should call M'ris
Salisbury this examin't answered yes if hee pleased presently after
the said Bonham was gone came Mr Richard Wright where this examin't
was & sate downe by her & asked this examin't to lye with her but
this examin't told him shee would not consent to any such thing the
sd Mr Wright swore hee must & would lye with her shee this examin't
desired him as he was a gen't to forbeare such incivilities yett - -
notwithstanding all this prevailed nothing but the sd Mr Wright throw
this Examin't downe & with struggling this examin'ts - (blotted here)-
clothing came of & gott upon this examin't by force & Ravished her &
shee cryed out twice as loud as shee could & told him what Law
would aforde her shee would not spare him in. imediatly after the
sd Mr Wright went into the weedes, Mr Willsford came presently after
this & asked this examin't if shee were alone Mr Wright heareing Mr
Willsford speake made answere & came out of the weedes & they two
went away together, presently came after Mr Clay Mr Horsley & James
Ashton with wine & asked this examin't to drinke but shee answered
them noe but one tooke her by one hand & another by the other hand
& dranke a health to him that laye with her last but shee this
examin't refused to drinke & as soone as shee had made ready her head
shee this Examin't went away & left the company & as she goeing by the
way mett w'th Mrs Salisbury & told her the sd M'ris Salisbury what bad
fortune had befalne her the sd examin't M'ris Salisbury answered &
said that Mr Wright was a gen't & that it was pitty: the sd Mrs
Salisbury bid this Examin't tarry there & shee would goe & call Mr
Wright soe when Mr Wright came Mrs Salisbury taxed him of the matter
at the first Mr Wright denied. it but after hee did not much stand out
in it & told this Examin't that if shee would make noe words of it &
be friends w'th him hee would give her satisfaction for the wrong hee
had done her And further this Examin't sayth not"

INDEX.

Abbott, Jno. 24. 25. 61. 106.
Adams, Wm. 53. 54. 55.
Aires, Jno. 17. 46.
Alderton, Isaac, Jr., 76.
Alexander, Robt. 12.
Allam see Allen.
Allen, Jahel, 112.
    Jane, 121. 122.
    Jeremy, 37. 90. 103.
    Tho. 12. 17.
    Wm. 63. 112. 121. 122.
Allenson, Walter, 90. 123.
    Walter, Jr. 90. 123.
Allenson, Wm. 67. 68. 72. 80.
    99. 103. 104. 118.
Allerson, Deborah and Wm. 58.
Anderson, David, 88
    Robt. 5.
Armorer, Jno. 4.
Armsbye, Jno. 109.
Ashton, Charles, 8. 14. 27.
    28. 29. 48. 111.
    Mrs. Charles. 28.
    James, 61. 130. 131.
    Ralph, 19.
Ashton-Barnes Case 27.
Atherton, Rich. 100
Atkinson, Alice, 62. 130.131.
    Robt. 15. 16. 90.
Atwell, Edw. 75. 76.
Austen, James. 69.

Backster, Tho. 29.
Bacon, Thos. 83.
    Wm. 103.
Bailes, Eliz & Jno. 9
    Tho. 103.
Baily, Mr. 78.
Baineham, Alex. 88. 114. 116.
Baker, Eliza. 32.
    Theodore, 41.
    Thomas, 88. 89.
Baldridge, Tho. 8. 21. 24. 52.
    83. 88. 89. 91. 99. 100.
Bales, Tho. 124.
Ball, Ann 44.
    Richd. 103.
Ballard, Tho. 32.
Barnes, Henry, 1. 11. 49. 107. 114.
Barnes, Jno. 27. 28. 62. 121.
Barrow, Margaret, 25.
Bashaw, Margaret, 112.

Bassett, Catherine, 92.
    Matthew, 6. 12.
    Tho. 16. 92.
    Sarah, 92.
    Susan, 92.
Batte, Captain Wm. 78. 79.
Batten, Wm. 70.
Bayles, Jno. 51. 67.
Baylor, Jno. 65.
Bayly, Arthur, 75.
    Mary, 54.
Bec, John, 105.
Beckett, Jno. 99.
Bedlam, - - 124.
    Elizabeth, 84.
    John, 5.
    Wm. 37. 40. 45. 78. 81. 89.
    Wm., Jr., 124.
    Mrs. Wm. 89.
Beesly, Wm. 120.
Bennett, - - "Goodman" 109.
    John, 14. 15. 27. 30. 67. 70
        90. 91. 111.
    Gov. Richd. 39. 71. 95. 102.
        104. 110. 123. 125. 127.
Berkeley, Sir William, 76. 77. 94.
        101. 103. 104. 108. 109
        110. 111. 116. 117. 121
        124. 127.
Berry, Francis, 29.
    George, 14. 51. 111. 118. 129.
Betts see Botts.
Billingsby, Major Jno. 15. 16. 90.
Biscoe, Jo 83.
Bishop, Cyprian, 20. 91. 103.
        His mischief making,
        96. 97.
Bishop, Sarah, 96.
Blagg, Tho. 20. 98.
Bland, Edward, 56.
Bloome, Bartholomew, 121.
Blunstone, Mary, 41.
Bolton, Mr. 16.
Boman, Mr. 52.
Bonham, Saml. 131.
Booth, Rob. 54.
Botts (Betts ?) William, 14. 32. 50.
    52. 85. 124.
Boulton, Francis. 92.
    Hugh, 92.
Bowyer, Andrew and Sarah, 20.
    Sarah, 96. 97.
Boyd, Thos. 88.
Boys, Tho. 109.

Brackitt, Mr. 1. 83.
Bradshaw, Jno. 8. 43. 68. 128.
    Robt. 27. 121.
Branch, Arthur, 7. 12. 14. 46. 47 77.
    John, Mary & Mary, Jr. 56
Brent, Edm. 14.
    Capt. Gyles, 12. 13. 21. 22 24. 25. 106.
    Margaret, 5. 21. 24. 25.
Brewer, Tho. 8. 33. 35. 36. 45. 46. 48. 53. 60. 126. 127. 128
Bridges, Hercules, 10. 14. 26. 106. 114.
Britton, Lyonell, 63.
Brodnax, Thos. 82. 100.
Brodhurst, Walter, 1. 2. 3. 8. 13 15. 18. 24. 40. 77. 90. 93. 97. 108. 109. 114. 115. 118. 120.
Brolett, Jane, 57.
Brooke, Henry. 2. 16. 20. 83. 90. 96. 114.
    Michael, 46. 50. 70. 92. 103.
Broughton, Tho. 50. 54. 67. 68. 72. 80. 86. 97. 105. 111. 112. 117. 120. 123. 126.
Browne, Jno. 100. 127.
    Richd. 116.
    Tho. 4.
Brunton, Tho. 7.
Bruster, Suck: 128.
Bryand an Irishman, 71.
Budd, Richd. 35. 40. 42. 45. 46. 51. 57. 59. 63. 64. 71. 73. 93. 103. 119. 122. 129.
    called Church Robber, 119.
    Mrs. Richd. 71.
Bullocke, Mr. 120.
Burbage, Capt. Tho. 55.
Burrell, Robt. 64. 126.
Burwell, Lewis. 2. 76. 77. 90.
    Brodhurst letter, 90.
Butler, Mr. (Ship Captain) 87.
    Thos. 5.
    Wm. 13.
Butt, Robt. 26. 106.
Byram, Abra. 27. 46. 47. 65. 66. 67. 70. 72. 75. 117. 118.
    Thos. 75.

Calfe, Jose. 127.
Calvert, Leonard, 25.
    Mrs. Mary, 39. 119.
    Mr. Sampson, 25. 30. 35. 39 42. 45. 107. 119.

Calvert's disagreement with the Puritans. 39.
Cammell, Jno. 4.
Carmichael, Geo. 49.
Carpenter, Philip. 34. 35. 36. 40. 42. 81. 91. 102. 117. 128.
Carter, Jno. 41.
Cartwright, Henry. 16. 54. 61. 66. 78. 117.
Carver, Wm. 64.
Castleton, Robt. 65.
Chaddocke, Mr. 83.
Chambers, Jno. 31. 102.
Chapman, Winter, 83. 115.
Chichester, Mr. 22. 48. 122.
Cingcleate, Edmund (Sinclair ?) 92.
Clapham, Wm. Senior, 31. 113.
Clayborne, Col. Wm. 39. 67. 72.
Clare, Richd. 8. 59. 62. 66. 98.
Claughton, James. 3. 9. 11. 20. 41 44. 46. 61. 62. 66. 68. 78. 82 89. 92. 94. 95. 108. 112.
Clay, Francis. 10. 18. 103. 130.
Clayborne, Col. William. 30. 33. 67 72. 82. 95. 102. 106. 108. 109. 110. 111. 114. 123. 124. 125. 127.
Clew, Jno. 56.
Cleows, Jno. 4.
Clever, Margaret. 23.
Clocker, Daniel, 29.
Cobra, Max. 41.
Cocke, Jeffery (the person referred to is doubtless Jeffery Gooch) 112
Cocke, Wm. 7. 8. 16. 19. 21. 25. 29. 83. 100. 121.
Coggin, Tho. 4. 14. 51. 64. 65. 67. 73. 86. 98. 103. 119.
Cololough, Geo. 7. 61. 69. 77. 89. 91. 102. 105. 116. 117. 121. 124. 129.
Cole, Martin. 19. 24. 32. 37. 46. 47. 48. 59. 60. 66. 67. 68. 124.
    Richard. 38. 41. 48. 109. 125.
Coles, Edward. 19. 32. 37. 60. 64. 72. 85. 105. 111. 113. 124.
    Mrs. Edward. 85.
    Matthew. 14.
Cole, Richard. 116. 118. 123.
    Robers. 114.
Colsecum (?) James. 7.
Compton, Ann. 25.
    John, Junior. 124.
Comsens, Jno. 92.
Conaway, Freeman, 61.
Conger, William. 54. 92.

Conyers, Tho. 70. 114.
Cooke, Jno. 21. 22. 29. 102.114.
    Myles, 7. 12. 77.
Cooper, Jeremy. 9. 18.
Corbell, Angell, Angell,Jr.;
    Anne, Clement, Gabriel,
    John. 25.
Cornelison, Cornelius, 105.
Cornewaleys, Capt. Thos. 22. 29. 100.
Cornish, Joan. 70.
    John. 113.
    Wm. 18. 55. 67.
Cotancau (or Cotancean ?) Jacob.
    6. 13. 20. 21. 23. 40. 107. 108.
    John. 24. 129.
Courtnell, Geo. 45. 46. 53. 54. 61. 62. 70. 72. 91. 120.
Cowell, Mr. 87.
Cox, Simon. 53. 60.
    Vincent. 38. 41. 48. 120.
Cristom, David. 12.
Cromwell, Gershon. 14. 113.
Crouch, Geo. 103.
Cunery, John. 97.
Curmickelle, Geo. 49.

Damorell, Laurence, 60.
Danby (Dandy) John, 7. 11. 21. 25. 29. 30. 31. 42. 78. 80. 100. 107. 113.
Danell (Dauell ?) Walter, 81.
Dankington, Thos. 44.
Dankly, Edw. 3.
Darrow, Thos. 48.
Dauell (Danell ?) 81.
Davies, Jno. 16. 26. 36. 42. 43. 49. 100. 111. 113. 118. 122. 125.
Dawson, William. 84.
Day, Geo. 17. 18. 115.
Dedman, Jno. 115. (see Dodman)
Dennis, Barbary. 12. 94.
    John. 3. 8. 12. 51. 78. 81. 109. 118.
    John, Senior. 45. 93. 94. 103.
    John, Junior. 93. 94.
    Pascoe. 108.
    Richard. 107.
Derickson, Jacob. 105.
Dicks, Mary. 29.
Digges, Gov. Edw. 72.
Dodman (Dedman) Jno. 16. 26.

Dodson, Gervase. 30. 31. 43 51.108. 110. 112. 115. 117. 125. 126. 129.
    His oath as surveyor. 108.
Dorrill, Elinor. 85.
    Thos. 85.
Douglas, Jno. 34.
    Robert. 72.
Douglas & Co., Capt. Wm. 69.
Donne, Walter. 7.
Draper, Jno. 120.
Dunkington, Tho. 112.
Dunn, Samuel. 23.

Eacles, Jno. 8.
Earle, Jno. 35. 44. 46. 55. 78. 111. 128.
    Mary. 128.
Edenborough, Andrew. 4.
Edmunds, Charles. 123.
Edwards, Christopher. 12.
    Edm. 121.
Edwire, Wm. 77.
Ellis. Thos. 117.
Elston, Ralph. 96.
Eltonhed, Wm. 100.
Essex, Jno. 2. 38. 77. 86. 98. 117. 120.
Evans, Robt. 129.

Faucett, Jno. 38.
Feild, Ann. 23.
Flepe, Cuthbert, 115. 116.
Fleet, Capt. Henry. 21.
Fletcher, Lt. Col. Geo. 1. 4. 15. 39. 40. 80. 93. 96. 97. 99. 103.
    His expense as burgess, 99.
Flint, Mrs. Dorothy. 38. 96.
Flint, Richard. 20. 31. 38. 45. 51. 52. 54. 61. 95. 96. 97. 103. 110. 111. 112. 113. 126.
Flippen, Peter, 109.
Ford, Mrs. 88.
Forshawes, Hugh. 75.
Foster, Mr. 80. 121.
    John. 11. 14. 65. 66. 67. 70. 112.
    Seth. 3. 44. 50. 55. 58. 60. 70. 122. 128.
Fouch, Hugh. 9. 15. 36. 90. 110.
Foxcroft, Daniel. 54. 126.
Freake, Wm. 8. 10. 20. 26. 30.
Freeman, Lt. Col. 39. 72. 123.
Frissell, Jno. 37.
Fulford, Humfrey, 42. 90.

Gamblin, Joan. 96.
       John. 60. 62. 81. 93.
         111. 127.
Garraed, Tho. 49.
Gaskins, Tho. 33. 45. 46. 51.
    106. 107. 121.
Gatehouse, Jno. 61. 68. 106.
Gassall, Thos. 26.
Gerrard, see Garrett.
Gerratt, Tho. 49. 65. 66. 77. 100
    114. 122.
Gibb, Richd. 59. 61.
Gibbins, Jno. (Gibbon ?) 57.
Gibble, Richd. 32. 45. 46. 69.
Gilbird, Rafe. 62.
Gilman, Lewes. 112.
Ginsey, Wm. 58. 128.
Glover, Daniel. 49.
Glower, Thos. 63.
Goche, Jeffery, 61. 104.
Godfrey, Jno. 41.
Gooch, Jeffery, 61. 104.
Gookin, Wm. 55.
Gossard, Tho. 2.
Gover, Edw. 63.
Gray, Francis. 4. 5. 8. 10. 13.
    14. 18. 20. 83. 88. 114.
    (the names Gray and Clay may
    possibly be confused in these
    old records.)
Gray, Joshua, son of Francis, 88.
Greensted see Grinsted.
Gresham, Jno. 4. 8. 13. 14. 19. 24.
    25. 27. 45. 51. 59. 61. 62.
    75. 81. 82. 86. 91. 93. 98. 103
    124.
        Justinian, 124.
Gribble see Gibble.
Grice (Jrice) Jno. 7.
Griffin, David. 56.
Grigson, Richd. 56.
Griggs, Mary. 7.
Grinsted, William. 122.
    Where he was caught in a
    jam. 130.
Gublin, Jno. 59.
Gundey, Jno. 11. 16.

Hailes, Hen. 112.
Hackett, Capt. Thos. 26. 31. 46.
    106. 113.
Haldich, Wm. 5.
Hale, Mr. & Mrs. 115.
    Geo. 67.
Haler, Hen. 78. 89. 123. 128.

Hales, Tho. 8. 9. 10. 35. 52. 54.
    56. 68. 82. 84. 89. 103. 111.
    113. 116. 124. 125.
Hall, Jno. 117.
Hallowes, John. 1. 2. 3. 4. 5. 8.
    10. 13. 15. 18. 19. 21. 22. 23
    35. 42. 48. 76. 83. 89. 93. 101
    102. 108. 114. 115. 120. 122.
Hamond, Jno. 17.
    Percy. 45. 65. 90. 102. 128.
Hampton, Jno. 4. 5. 82. 83. 88.
Handy, Jno. 76. 82.
Haney, Jacob Simonson, 12.
Hansworth, Francis, 128.
Hardich, Wm. 22. 44. 54. 82. 83.
    96. 109.
Harding, Wm. 69.
Harrison, Isaac. 127.
        Joseph, 105.
Harwood, Angell. 107.
Hawkins, Jno. 75.
    Richd. 2. 4. 77. 78. 96.
    Thomas. 3. 4. 7. 8. 14.
    16. 30. 31. 35. 36. 37. 39. 44.
    50. 54. 56. 60. 62. 68. 75. 76.
    77. 78. 79. 80. 86. 97. 113.
    116. 119. 122.
Hawkins, Mrs. Thos. 80. 97.
Hawley, James. 52. 57. 73. 64. 66.
    125.
    Mrs. James. 71.
    Tho. (Orlye ?) 25. 27.
Hayles, Jno. 62. 84.
Haynie. John. 6. 8. 9. 11. 12. 13.
    20. 27. 34. 40. 50. 51. 52. 55.
    59. 62. 64. 68. 69. 70. 72. 80.
    83. 89. 90. 105. 110. 112. 122.
    130.
Hayward, Nicholas. 11. 18. 45. 60
    87. 88.
    His letter. 87.
Heinemann, Charles B. 81.
Hellen, Natha. 107.
Henley, Edw. 34. 42. 53. 65. 102.
    118. 123. 127.
    Joan. 118.
    John. 43.
Hennibourne, Robt. 89.
Hewes, Richd. 3.
Hickman, Avis. 58.
    Nath. 31. 44. 58. 111.
    122. 128.
Higgins, Mr. 98. 103. 106.
    Geo. 82. 84.
Higginson, Col. 123.
Hill, Capt. 83.

Hill, Col. Edw. 72.
    John. 107.
        Richd. 114. 121.
Hillard, Mr. 114.
Hiller, Mr. 83.
Hillyers, John. 89. 109.
Hinman, Jno. 101.
Hodge, Jno. 105.
Holden, Richard. 26. 36. 44. 46.
    57. 59. 64. 88. 106. 109. 111
    112. 123. 128.
Holland, Dan. 70. 72.
    Joyce. 70.
Holling, Nath. 75.
Honiborne, Robt. 9. 10. 84.
Hopkins, Tho. 33. 37. 46. 51. 97
    126. 127.
Hopkins, Wm. 120.
Hopper, Jno. 32. 59. 60. 61.
Horsley, Mr. 131.
    Jane. 80.
    Joseph. 121.
    Ralph. 5. 7. 8. 12. 14.
    20. 27. 29. 53. 60. 64. 72. 77
    79. 80. 81. 86. 91. 92. 101.
    116. 120. 121. 128.
Howard, Jno. 11. 46.
Howell, Jno. 65.
Hubard, Ro. 39. 123. 127.
Hudson, Edw. 1. 2. 7. 10. 11. 60
    100.
Hulet, Hannah. 32.
    John. 31. 32. 33. 50. 104. 106
Hull, Augustine. 106.
    Edwd. 31. 50.
    John. 23. 43. 52. 55. 64. 70
    110. 111. 128.
    Richard. 23.
Hunt, Nath. 7.
Hurst, Henry. 3. 66. 75. 93. 120.
Husband, Mr. 119.
    Richd. 87.

Indians. Order regarding Arms. 15
Ingle, Capt. Richd. 100
Ingram, Eliza. 126.
    Mrs. Jane. 126.
    Jane, Junior. 126.
    John. 7. 31. 41. 78. 79.
    109. 110. 126.
    Thomas. 126.
Jackson, Barnaby. 100.
Jackson, Wm. 89.
Jacob, Francis. 66.
Jansson, Abraham. 105.

Jarvis, Francis. 77.
Jelles. Thomas the younger. 84.
Jenkins, Jno. 102. 114.
Jerman, Abraham. 21. 102.
Johnson, Henry. 5.
    John. 26. 66. 105.
Jones, Mr. 123.
    Franc. 25.
    Nathaniel. 83. 89.
    Tho. 7.
    William. 56. 61.
Jorden, Capt. 79.
Jrice, Jno. 7.
Jernew, Nicholas. 64.

Kaye. Jno. 60. 72.
Kedby, Tho. 30. 63. 104. 105. 108.
    110. 116. 124.
Kedyer, Thos. 30.
Kelly, Jno. 5. 84.
Keene, Mrs. Mary. 22. 92.
    Matthew. 91.
    Susan. 22. 91.
    Tho. 1. 22. 81. 91. 92.
    Thomas, Junior. 91. 92.
    William. 22. 91.
Kent. Jno. 8. 44. 46. 53. 58. 90.
    109. 128.
    Phebe. 27.
Kingwell, Helen. 75.
    Sarah. 59. 65. 66.
    Thos. 36. 59. 65. 66.
    75. 86. 93. 111. 121.
Knight. Isaac. 4. 78. 116.
    John. 92. 120.
    Peter. 34. 36. 38. 42. 56.
    60. 61. 66. 67. 69. 99. 106. 109.
    111. 117. 124. 126. 130.
Knight, Thos. 10. 18. 19. 38. 44.
    89. 102.
Knight, Capt. Wm. 6. 121.
Knott see Nott.

Lake, Richd. 105.
Lambdon, Robt. 39. 42. 45. 68. 112.
    117. 120. 121.
Larrett, Jno. 55. 81.
Laud. Robt. 29. 66. 125. 128.
Layton, Judith. 23.
Lee, Hannah. 27. 28. 62.
Lee. Hugh. 5. 14. 161 17. 22. 26.
    27. 31. 34. 37. 45. 46. 50. 52.
    56. 57. 58. 61. 63. 64. 65. 67.
    72. 77. 78. 80. 82. 84. 89. 91.
    93. 99. 100. 101. 102. 103. 108.
continued.

Lee, Hugh. Continued. 111. 112.
    113. 121. 124. 127. 128.
        Sworn Com'r. 57.
        Exp. as Burgess. 99.
Lee, Jno.   24. 106.
    Robt. 124.
Lewes, Wm. 3.
Lewis, Mr. 123.
Light, Wm. 54. 124.
Lindsaye, Rev. David. 69.
Lindsey, Wm. 4. 29.
Linton, Anth. 35. 45. 48. 50. 54.
    56. 62. 64. 104. 117. 125.
    128. 129.
Little, Wm. 52. 61. 70. 126.
Lloyd, Mr. Richd. 18. 45.
Lodell, Timothy. 117.
Lonedon, (London ?) Wm. 17.18.19
Loning, Saml. 84.
Lowe, Robt. 48.
Ludlow, Col. Geo. 39. 123.
Lumpkin, Thos. 59.
Lund, Thos. 45. 60. 83.

Macgregger, James. 30. 39. 49. 54
    83. 110. 124.
Margreggor, Moriall, 119.
Machywax, Indian King. 68.
Maddox, Rice. 6. 36. 77. 89.
Magdoull, Alex. 43.
Maidwell, Thos. 78.
Makewater, Max. 49.
Manesfry, Fra. 100.
Maning. Jacob. 113.
        John. 99.
        Joseph. 29. 38. 48. 119.
            122.
Marsh, Geo. 126.
Marshall, Jno. 7.
Mason, Geo. 14.
Matthews, Saml. 11.
        Thos. 22.
May. Ann.   38.
    David.   5.
Mayes, Hen. 59. 62. 129.
Meares, Mary. 41.
Mecham, Tho.   23.
Medcalf see Metcalf.
Meeks, Jno. 117.
Meels, Daniel. 14. 20.
Meriwether, Nicholas. 72.
Meroll, Jno. 41.
Merrey, James. 41.
Metcalf, (Medcalf) Wm. 51. 55.
    91. 120.

Michael, Jno. 31. 50. 105.111.123.
Minefee, Geo. 104.
Moone, Abraham. 58. 104. 114.
Moore, Ann and Ann Junior. 41.
    Edward. 41. 49.
    Walt. 23.
Morris, Nicholas. 1. 8. 15. 19. 24
    29. 34. 39. 41. 43. 45. 46. 47.
    48. 50. 51. 52. 57. 64. 65. 67.
    69. 70. 73. 85. 98. 103. 106.
    112. 118. 119. 122. 127. 131.
        Mrs. Nicho. Morris. 47.71.
Morris-Cole-Wicher brawl. 46. 47.
Mosely, Hen. 20. 27. 46. 53. 55.
    91. 92. 127.
        Henry, Junior. 75.
        John. 75.
        William. 1.
Motley, John. 124.
Motteram, Jno. 62.
Mottershed, Samuel (Perhaps an
    assumed name) 87. 88.
Mottrom, Frances. 124.
Mottrom, Colonel John. 1. 5. 6. 8.
    13. 15. 16. 19. 21. 24. 25. 29.
    30. 32. 33. 34. 36. 37. 41. 45.
    46. 48. 49. 51. 52. 54. 55. 56.
    57. 59. 60. 63. 67. 68. 71. 73.
    75. 80. 81. 82. 86. 89. 90. 91.
    91. 97. 99. 105. 113. 115. 116.
    118. 121. 124. 125. 129.
Mottrom, John, Junior. 116.
Munroe, Andrew. 4.
Myles. Jno. 17. 19. 20.

Napleton, Jacob. 127.
Nash, Mrs Ann. 41.
    Wm. 41. 43. 47. 48. 52. 57.
    59. 63. 64. 73. 126. 127.
Nash, Mrs. William. 64.
Newberry, Wm. 12.
Newman, Mr. 30.
        Elizabeth. 55.
        John. 80.
        Robert. 56. 64. 66. 67. 68.
            80.
        William. 117. 121.
Nicholls, Richd. 87. 88. 102.
        Samuel. 25. 110.
        William. 83.
Nott, Eliza. 129.
Nott, Geo. 45. 60. 62. 64. 72. 99.
    111. 117. 124. 129.

Odyer, Gabriel. 11. 16. 97. 113.
Orlye, Tho. 25. 27. 49. 92. 107.
116. 120.
Oversea, Simon. 90.
Owen, Jane. 71.

Packer, Jane. 84.
Paine, Jno. 16. 92.
Pakes, Walter. 17. 120.
Pare, Goodman 99.
Parker, Charles. 23.
Parks, Tho. 56.
Parry, Ann. 37.
Wm. 79.
Parse (Percy ?) John. 72.
Passep-an Indian. 113.
Peare, Jno. 8.
Pearce, Thos. 41. 43.
Pedell see Podell.
Peirce, Beardit. 84.
James. 25.
Capt. Wm. 53. 104.
Percy, Jno. (?) 72.
Perry, Andrew. 80.
Eliza, Jane Jr. Margaret,
80
Perry, Edmond. 36.
Jane. 9. 80. 81.
John, orphans of 127.
Wm. 80.
Pettitt, Jno. 41.
Pettus, Col. Tho. 72. 123.
Pew. Mr. 125.
Phelps, Cuthbert (ffelpe) 115.118.
Phillips, David. 104. 116.
John. 80.
Michael. 3.
Thomas. 3. 48.
Philp, Tho. 112.
Philpott, Thos. 29. 61. 72. 78.
99. 102. 112.
Pickard, Nicholas. 82.
Pites, Jno. 84.
Pitt, Henry. 84.
John. 84. 109.
Robt. 17. 84.
Playce, Jno. 124.
Mary. 124.
Podle, Corbet (Pedle, Pydle etc.)
2. 3. 13. 14. 15. 23. 24. 26.
44. 50. 55. 86. 90. 91. 108.
114.
Poole, Henrico. 79.

Pope, Nathaniel. 3. 8. 9. 11. 12.
13. 17. 18. 20. 21. 22. 29. 76.
83. 87. 88. 89. 98. 100.102.114.
Hayward letter 87.
Porter, Wm. 33.
Posley, Margaret. 4.
Potts, Patrick. 13.
Powell, John. 1. 2. 10. 25. 29. 42.
46. 48. 64. 66. 68. 80. 89. 102.
112. 122.
Poythers, Capt. 83.
Presly, Peter. 45.
Presly, William. 8. 9. 14. 15. 18.
29. 33. 34. 36. 41. 48. 49. 55.
59. 60. 62. 64. 65. 67. 68. 70.
72.80. 83. 95. 99. 119.123.124
Sworn High Sheriff 48.
Expense as Burgess 99.
Price, Howell. 70.
Pricce, Wm . 57.
Prichard, Walter. 56.
Prichett, Tho. 50. 59. 62. 67. 96.
Tho. Jr. 126.
Prosser, Jno. 48. 52. 57. 60. 127.
Pulford, Tho. 127.
Purnell, Mary. 50. 85.
Pydell see Podle.

Radford, Jno. 32. 37. 42. 43. 48.
52. 59. 61. 62. 67. 124. 125.
Exempt from Levy 61.
Ranon, Jno. 9.
Raughton, Wm. 97.
Raven, Jno. 54. 90.
Rawlings, Jno. 65.
Raymond, Richd. 59. 69.
Rayner, Henry. 3. 20. 25. 51. 52.
90. 91. 92. 120.
Reade, Archibald. 25.
Eliz. 71.
Sarah. 49.
Tho. 47. 52. 1291
Reynolds, Ann. 106.
James. 123.
Reynolds, William. 4. 7. 8. 14. 16.
20. 29. 43. 44. 45. 52. 81. 86.
92. 97. 98. 125.
Reynolds, Wm. Jr. 123.
Rhoden, Matthew. 8. 13. 14. 20. 27.
49. 52. 57. 63. 64. 71. 72. 73.
82. 91. 92. 108. 113. 124.
Rice, Richd. 62.
Rice, Thos. 26. 108.

Richardson, Elias. 98. 103. 106. 107.
Richardson, Simon. 6. 8. 9. 20. 24. 31. 37. 62. 70. 72. 85. 91. 103. 105.
    His malicious gossip 85.
Roberts, Christopher. 123.
    Daniel. 122.
    Edward (Everard) 44. 52. 112. 122. 123.
Roberts, Mrs Katherine. 66.
    Tho. 7.
Robinson, Cornelius. 81.
Rocke, Mrs Katherine. 27. 28.
    Henry. 20. 36. 37. 72. 77. 91. 112. 115.
Rocke, John. 91. 117.
Rogers, Eliza. 125.
    John. 125. 126.
    John, Jr. 125.
    Katherine 125.
    Thos. 10. 26.
Rogers, Capt. John. 57. 63. 64. 71. 72. 94. 101.
Rookewood, Jno. 12.
Roper, James. 114.
    Capt. Wm. 101.
Rosier, Jno. 2. 13. 19. 22. 76. 92. 93. 102. 108.
Rowse, Charles. 7.
Rumsey, Thos. 96.
Ryall, Edw. 114.
    Rebecca. 102.

Saffell, Thos. 16. 29. 55. 57. 106.
Salisbury, Isobel. 51. 130. 131.
    Isobel & Thos. 45. 47
    Thos. 126.
Sampson see Simpson.
Sampson, Mr. 30.
    John. 31. 112. 121.
    Paul. 122.
Sayer, Lydia. 63.
Scoggin, Thos. 47.
School. Free School ordered.16.
Sedgrave, Robt. 23. 83.
Selliack, Mr. 48. 119. 122.
Sentence, Henry. 25.
Sharp, Robt. 24. 35. 41. 46. 49. 57. 67. 117. 121. 123. 125. 126. 128.
Shaw, Alice. 56. 125. 128.
    Thomas. 50. 52. 54. 62. 125. 129.
Sheppard, Jno. 79.

Sheapard, Tho. 20. 31. 35. 42. 44. 54. 95. 111. 112. 122.
Silvester, Phillip. 26. 90. 91.
Simons, Francis. 15. 23. 25. 49. 53. 57. 58. 81. 92.
Simonson, Jacob. 31. 50.
Simpson see Sampson.
Simpson, Paul. 42. 45. 120.
Sinclair see Cingcleate ?
Sincler, Edmond. 108. 121.
Smith. Ann. 9. 62.
    Henry. 111
    Herbert. 8.
    John. 92. 123.
    Capt. John 121.
    Robt. 4. 9. 45. 46. 62. 123. 125
Smith, Sam. 1. 7. 8. 11. 13. 15. 25. 26. 40. 41. 47. 48. 50. 52. 55. 56. 57. 63. 64. 67. 71. 72. 80. 99. 100. 102. 114. 125.
Smyth, Rich. 23.
    Sarah. 62.
    William. 123.
    Zeph: 83. 96.
Sorcery and Witchcraft Case. 69.
Southorne, Judith and Sarah. 53.
Span, Hannah. 56.
    Richd. 10. 14. 18. 31. 37. 56. 64. 80. 86. 113.
Speke, Mrs. Ann. 115.
Speke, Thos. 1. 3. 7. 8. 9. 11. 12. 13. 15. 17. 21. 22. 36. 42. 45. 77. 78. 81. 83. 88. 89. 96. 99. 109. 114. 115. 116. 118.
    Expense as Burgess 99.
Spencer, Judith. 20.
Spense, Wm. 15.
Spicer, Wm. 42. 72. 67. 68. 86. 112. 118. 119. 126.
Spiller, David. 27. 36. 42. 45. 46. 51. 53. 59. 62. 91. 109. 112. 118. 119. 121. 122.
    His mischief making gossip 112
Squibb, Jno. 5. 37. 45. 53. 77. 97. 115. 116. 118.
Stafford, Robt. 41.
Stanley, Alice. 107.
    John. 29. 92. 116. 120.
Starkey, Mr. 55.
Stephens, Thos. 50. 85.
Stepping, Daniel. 75.
    Eliza. 75.
    Jonathan, 8. 50.
Steyne, Jos. 105.
Stoane, Benj. 87.
Stone, Capt. Wm. 100. 101.
Stranger, Mr. 105.

Stratford, Mary and Wm. 62.
Street, Woodhull. 85.
Stuart, Henry.
Sturman, Jno. 100.
Such, Robt. 62. 72.
Sudbery, Edw. 41.
Suningberke, Florintino. 30. 113.
Swaile, Rob. 56.
Swanley, Capt. 56.
Swanson, Jno. 107.

Tainler, Michael. 38. 83.
Tavernor, Gyles. 26. 106.
Taylor, Col. Wm. 123. 128.
Tempest, Edw. 11. 17. 22. 93.
Tennis, Justinian. 116.
Tew, Jno. 52. 108. 109.
Thackle, Jno. 125.
Thomas, Mrs. Frances. 37.
Thomas, William. 6. 9. 14. 16. 20
  26. 30. 31. 32. 33. 37. 38.
  41. 44. 45. 46. 48. 50. 52.
  61. 62. 63. 64. 68. 72. 84.
  85. 104. 105. 106. 111. 113.
  118. 123. 126. 128.
Thompson, Edw. 2. 4. 5. 8. 14.
  77. 78. 83. 96.
Thompson, Geo. 78.
  John. 7.
  Makum, 5.
  Richard. 82.
Thurston, Mr. (Sea Captain) 87.
Tingey, John and his family. 116.
  118.
Titherton, Rich. 128.
Trussell, Eliza. 108.
Trussell, John. 1. 6. 8. 9. 11.
  12. 14. 15. 17. 18. 21.
  24. 28. 29. 31. 32. 33.
  34. 35. 41. 48. 60. 62.
  64. 71. 82. 84. 92. 95.
  99. 103. 106. 108. 121.
    Expense as Burgess 99.
Trussell, Mrs. Mary. 108.
Toogood, Edw. 56.
Toppin, Henry. 84. 104. 123.
Trewett, Geo. 126.
Tuck, Robt. 112.
Tulney, Mr. 19.
Turney, Richard. 1. 2. 3. 6. 7.
  11. 15. 18. 19. 20. 21.
  23. 24. 25. 30. 31. 38.
  76. 103. 104. 107. 110.
  116. 121.

Vallins, James. 7.
Vane, Capt. 105.
Vaulx, Robt. 54. 123. 126.
VESTRYMEN   64.
Vincent, Henry. 109. 122.
  Wm. 38. 40. 109. 110.

Waddy, Jno. 4. 19. 20. 21. 51. 53.
  98. 109. 110. 126.
Wade, Wm. 56.
Waggell, Thos. 96.
Waldron, Dr. 101.
Wale (or Hale) Geo. 124.
Walker, Edw. 124.
  John. 34. 44. 62. 88. 122.
    128.
Walker, Richd. 42. 91.
  Wm. 109.
Walter, Thos. 58. 62.
Walton, Jno. 1. 2. 38. 46. 48. 76.
  102. 119. 120.
Warde, Wm. 128.
Warder, Wm. 38. 101.
Warre, Jno. 80.
Warell, Jno. 101.
Warrev, Mr. 56.
Warwell, Wm. 56.
Watson, Thos. 25.
Watts, Geo. 3. 6.
Weaver, Isaac. 107.
Webber, Mr. (Ship Captain) 87.
Weekes, Walter. 28. 30. 36. 46. 52.
  62. 90. 104. 123.
Wesson, Mary. 49.
West, Mr. 21.
  Eliza. 121.
  Henry and Thomas. 115.
  Capt. Jno. 70.
Westgate, Adam. 50 69.
Wheatley, Mrs. of Accomac. 101
White, Richd. 16. 27. 31. 43. 80. 84.
  90. 91. 97.
Whitley. William. 6. 12.
Whittington, Wm. 105.
Whitty, Capt. 79.
Wicher, Henry. 19. 24. 42. 46. 47.
  51. 126.
Wicks, Joseph. 36. 118.
Wife, John. 122.
Wildey (Willday) William. 14. 52.
  86. 103. 117.
    Deposition showing age. 86.
Wiles, Wm. 49.
Wilkinson, Mr. 82.

Wilkinson, Thos. 55. 76.
Willance, Christopher, 86.
Willis, Francis. 13.
Willis, James. 2. 9. 10. 27. 46.
    72. 109. 112. 123.
Willis, John. 56.
Wilsford, Bridgett. 120.
Wilsford, Thomas. 4. 5. 6. 7. 8.
    11. 13. 16. 36. 42. 43. 45.
    49. 53. 58. 60. 61. 75. 76.
    77. 84. 90. 91. 94. 99. 100.
    101. 102. 104. 109. 110. 116.
    118. 120. 121. 122. 123. 124.
    125. 126. 127. 128. 130. 131.
Wilson, Jno. 4.
Williams, Charles. 9. 15.
Woodes, Charles. 104.
Wright, Gyles. 75.
    John. 4.
    Richard. 62. 129. 130. 131.
Wright, Richard. Attack on his
    character. 130. 131.
Wood, Elizabeth. 32.
Woodridge, Mary. 12.
Wraughton, Wm. (Raughton) 97.
Wyard, Robt. 3. 13. 17. 20. 92.
Wyatt, Sir Francis. 104.

Yeardley, Argoll. 100. 104.
Yeo, Robt. 126.
Youlle, Thos. (Ewell). 3. 4. 6. 12.
    17. 19. 35. 51. 67. 77. 83.
    96.
Young, Reynold. 7.
Young, Thomas. 75. 76. 109.

www.ingramcontent.com/pod-product-compliance
Lightning Source LLC
Chambersburg PA
CBHW020655300426
44112CB00007B/393